Life and Death in Healthcare Ethics

In a world of rapid technological advances, the moral issues raised by life and death choices in healthcare remain obscure. *Life and Death in Healthcare Ethics: A Short Introduction* provides a concise, thoughtful and extremely accessible guide to these moral issues.

Helen Watt examines, using real-life cases, a range of choices taken by health professionals, patients and clients which lead to the shortening of life. The topics considered include:

- euthanasia and withdrawal of treatment
- the persistent vegetative state
- abortion
- IVF and cloning
- life-saving treatment of pregnant women

Clearly-written and insightful, *Life and Death in Healthcare Ethics* presupposes no prior knowledge of philosophy. It will be of interest to anyone approaching healthcare ethics for the first time, or seeking to develop his or her understanding of some core topics in the field.

Helen Watt is Research Fellow at the Linacre Centre for Healthcare Ethics in London.

D0162015

LONDON AND NEW YORK

Life and Death in Healthcare Ethics

A short introduction

Helen Watt

ROUTLEDGE

First published 2000
by Routledge
11 New Fetter Lane, London
EC4P 4EE

Simultaneously published in the USA
and Canada
by Routledge
29 West 35th Street, New York,
NY 10001

*Routledge is an imprint of the Taylor &
Francis Group*

Typeset in Times by Taylor & Francis
Books Ltd

Printed and bound in Great Britain by
Clays Ltd, St Ives PLC

*British Library Cataloguing in
Publication Data*
A catalogue record for this book is
available from the British Library

*Library of Congress Cataloging in
Publication Data*
A catalogue record for this book has
been requested

ISBN 0–415–21573–0 (hbk)
ISBN 0–415–21574–9 (pbk)

Contents

Acknowledgements

In writing this book, I have been generously helped by the following people: John Berry, Stratford Caldecott, Alison Davis, Peter Doherty, Janet Doyle, Anthony Fisher, Clarissa Fleischer, Germain Grisez, Colin Harte, Michael Jarmulowicz, Ian Jessiman, John Kelly, John Keown, Jacqueline Laing, Mette Lebech, Matthew McDonald, Annette Menouar, Neil Murray, Rupert Obholzer, Paul Robinson and Paul Watt. I am particularly indebted to those who read more than one draft of the manuscript: Luke Gormally, Birgit Jentsch, Rachel McDonald and Ted Watt. I am grateful to Tony Bruce and Lia Zografou of Routledge for their advice and support, and to three Routledge referees for many helpful suggestions. For all remaining errors, I am, of course, wholly responsible.

Finally, I would like to thank Jozef Glasa for permission to use material which first appeared in *Medical Ethics and Bioethics*, and in J. Glasa and J. R. Klepanec (eds) (1998) *Healthcare Under Stress: Moral Integrity in Time of Scarcity*, Bratislava: Institute of Medical Ethics and Bioethics.

Introduction

Healthcare ethics is in the news, and seems likely to remain so. Hardly a week goes by without a new case coming up for discussion by the media. Frozen embryos, euthanasia of brain-damaged patients, the use of foetal tissue in research – a seemingly endless series of cases are reported in response to a growing public interest. Cloning, for example, is an issue in this area which – not surprisingly – has received enormous attention from the media and society at large.

Yet with all this interest in new cases, the moral issues raised will often remain obscure. Many people, including health professionals, will find themselves more or less perplexed when confronted with the latest problem case. Even if they feel strongly that a certain position is the right one to take with regard to the case in question, they may be unsure why they feel this way, or how their position might be rationally defended.

The role of emotion

The term 'yuk factor' has been used to describe a reaction of repugnance to some particular proposal. For example, many people reacted with horror to the proposal that eggs from female aborted foetuses be used in *in vitro* fertilization. Again, many people react with unease or distaste to the notion of keeping someone alive indefinitely in a 'persistent vegetative state'.

Such instinctive reactions are often criticized as 'emotive'. The role of emotion in our moral judgements is not, however, a simple matter. Moral judgements cannot be reduced to emotional reactions devoid of any content: by saying 'this is wrong', I do not simply mean to describe, or express, my emotions at this time. However, it is certainly true that our moral judgements are often accompanied by, and influenced by, emotional reactions of some kind. Spontaneous reactions and judgements may initiate a reasoned exploration of the problem, which will sometimes confirm the appropriateness of our original response. Alternatively, such an exploration may fail to confirm the appropriateness of the reaction first evoked.

How, then, should we regard our own spontaneous reactions to moral problems? If such problems do, in fact, have objective solutions,[1] however hard these are to find, it may be the case that our spontaneous reactions point the way to these solutions. On the other hand, our reactions may mislead us – because, for example, they are biased by our wish to defend what we ourselves want to do, or have done in the past, in response to similar problems.

In many cases, if not in all cases, spontaneous reactions should neither be discounted nor simply accepted without investigation as morally appropriate. Rather, they should spur us on to find their rational basis, if any, in some aspect of the case at hand. If we are unable to find such a basis, this does not mean that there is none to be found. However, it does mean that we are less likely to be able to convince those whose judgements and reactions are different from our own.

The purpose of this book

What can be offered in the way of reasons for taking a particular position with regard to moral problems[2] in healthcare? In this book, I will set forward, and defend against objections, the approach I myself find most helpful to a series of such problems. The approach I will defend links morality to human fulfilment: to the enjoyment of 'basic human goods' such as life, knowledge and friendship. It gives a central place to human intentions in evaluating means for promoting human well-being. It lays stress on the impact of choices on the agent him- or herself: on the kind of people we make ourselves to be by choosing as we do. There is, I will argue, more to morality than the achievement of good results – to say nothing of 'the best' of all the results we could achieve. While the expected results of our actions are often decisive in judging them right or wrong, we should not attempt to judge our actions simply on the basis of the outcome they produce.

This book is intended as a brief introduction to the ethics of healthcare, in relation to life-and-death issues in particular. It has been written with both the general reader and students and professionals in medicine, nursing, law, philosophy and related areas in mind. The approach is one of 'natural' philosophy: there are no religious premises in the arguments put forward or discussed. In a book of this size, it is impossible to do more than sketch out arguments which could be expounded at far greater length. Moreover, I have chosen to focus on life-and-death issues – abortion, euthanasia, 'letting die', and so on – rather than on more mundane but also important concerns such as confidentiality and informed consent. Other concerns mentioned only in passing are those involving human reproduction: that is, the generation of human lives, as opposed to the treatment of existing human lives. Such concerns will perhaps be addressed in more detail in a future publication. In any case, my hope is that readers with an interest in healthcare ethics will be encouraged by this book to explore in depth those aspects of the subject which they find most interesting.

Chapter 1

Homicide
Moral approaches

The Arthur case

On 28 June 1980, a child with Down's syndrome was born in Derby City Hospital. The parents on hearing from the midwife that there were signs of Down's were shocked and distressed, and said they did not want the child. After confirming the diagnosis, Dr Arthur, a consultant paediatrician, wrote on the records: 'Parents do not wish baby to survive. Nursing care only'. The child, named John Pearson, was given water but no food; he was also given very high doses of DF118, a pain-killing drug. John Pearson died on the fourth day after his birth.

Dr Arthur was charged at first with murder, on the grounds that the child was given ten times the therapeutic dose of DF118 and put on 'nursing care only' with the intention that he die. One witness observed that uncomplicated Down's is not, in any case, a painful condition for which pain-killing drugs would be required. However, another witness argued, from the evidence of the autopsy, that death might have been

caused by birth defects in the child unknown to Dr Arthur at the time he gave orders for his treatment. The charge of murder was withdrawn and Dr Arthur was charged with attempted murder: a charge of which he was eventually acquitted by the jury.

Witnesses called for the defence maintained – rightly or wrongly – that what Dr Arthur had done was standard medical practice. These witnesses included Sir Douglas Black, then President of the Royal College of Physicians, who stated that where parents did not wish their Down's child to live it was 'ethical to terminate life', providing certain factors, such as the ability of the parents to cope and give the child a happy life, were taken into account. Black observed that it was good medical practice to distinguish between allowing to die and killing, although he conceded that this distinction was 'somewhat difficult to defend in logic' (Gormally 1994: 106).

'Killing' and 'letting die'

The Arthur case raises a number of moral questions, a selection of which we will be looking at in turn. To begin with, is there any foundation for the claim that 'letting die' – say, by omitting to feed – is significantly different from 'killing' – say, by administering a drug? While not, perhaps, satisfactory as it stands, the claim has a certain plausibility in some situations. There do seem to be cases in which the distinction between causing death by positive action and allowing death to happen has some moral relevance. To alter the world in a way which does harm is something which seems to need more justification than leaving the world the way it is, with the result that harm occurs. To push someone on to a busy road, for example, seems harder to justify than failing to pull someone off the road, even if other factors such as risks and burdens for those involved remain the same.

In what kind of case does the act/omission distinction – and/or the causing/allowing distinction[1] – not seem morally significant? It is certainly very much more difficult to argue that these distinctions are morally significant where death is *intended* by the person who is 'acting' or 'not acting'.[2] In a case where the moral verdict is uncontroversial – a straightforward case of murder for gain, for example – it does not seem that there is a moral difference between bringing about death by 'positive act', and bringing it about by omission. Take the case of someone who deliberately lets a child drown in order to obtain a legacy (say, after watching him slip in the bath).[3] Here we have both a moral duty to act in order to save the child's life and an intention to bring about death by omitting to do so. Is this not morally comparable to pushing the child underwater to achieve the same end – that is, the death of the child?

Role of intention

In looking at such cases, we need to examine the role of *intention* in determining what a person does. It is important to realize that actions are not just physical events,[4] or non-events: *intentions make the action*. Imagine two people sitting beside the child drowning in the bathtub while they fail to intervene. These people may look similar from the outside, but may have different intentions and thus be doing, at the moral level, two quite different things. One may be intending that the child die, while the other may simply be afraid to intervene[5] (because, say, the murderer has threatened to kill him if he does). Such a person is saying to himself 'I won't intervene, because if I do this other person will kill me'. The other person is saying to himself 'I won't intervene *so that the child will die*, and I can inherit the money'.

There is, it seems, a difference which can be morally significant between *intending* someone's death and *accepting* someone's death. To say this is not to say that cases of the second kind will always be morally preferable to cases of the first. The person who lets a child drown out of a dislike of getting wet may be acting no less wrongly than the person who lets a child drown with the intention of bringing about his death. However, if the first way of acting is wrong it is wrong for *different reasons* from the second way of acting. It is a case of callous negligence, rather than deliberate infanticide.

The outward behaviour of a person will often involve a whole cluster of intentions, all of which will need to be justifiable in order to justify what is done. For example, the person who lets the child drown may be intending to sit on a chair, to leave the child in the water, to ensure the child drowns, to inherit the money, to support his family with the money he inherits, and so on. The fact that some intentions are in themselves neutral (for example, the intention to sit on a chair) or in themselves good (for example, the intention to support one's family) is clearly not sufficient to justify behaviour of this kind. For what we do to be morally acceptable, not just some but *all* our intentions must be morally acceptable.

A case of euthanasia?

So did Dr Arthur's behaviour involve an acceptable cluster of intentions? The problematic intentions in his case are, of course, the intention to prevent the child being fed (assuming this was part of what was meant by 'nursing care only'), the intention to have him given DF118 in high doses, and the intention (or presumed intention) to bring death about by those means. Other intentions, such as Dr Arthur's intention to write on the records or to spare the child suffering, are in themselves uncontroversial.

The Arthur case would appear to be one of euthanasia, or attempted euthanasia, since Dr Arthur appears to have acted as he did with the aim of ending the life of the child. Both those who defend euthanasia and those who oppose it will often accept that euthanasia can be carried out either by act or by omission (Harris 1995; Finnis 1995). If the aim is to bring about death, it is euthanasia whether this is done by an omission (such as failure to feed or to cancel an order *not* to feed) or by a 'positive act' (such as an overdose, or orders for an overdose). If we assume that Dr Arthur gave the orders he did because he believed that the life of John Pearson *would not be worthwhile* then his giving those orders seems to satisfy entirely the following definition of euthanasia: *an act or omission intended to bring about death on the grounds that life is not worth living* (Gormally 1994: 10–11).

Having an interest

Was it the case that John Pearson's life was in fact not worth living? To put it another way,[6] was life or continued existence in John Pearson's interests?

There are those who argue that *no* newborn baby – disabled or otherwise – has an interest, or an interest of 'personal' significance, in continuing to live (Tooley 1983: 117–20, 410–12; Singer 1993: 96–9, 131). This is because a baby is incapable of having a concept of his or her life, and hence of wanting that life to continue. A baby is also incapable of other long-term desires, which would be thwarted if he or she did not survive. While babies (it is said) may have interests in avoiding pain, since they are capable of wanting the pain to stop, they have no interest in survival, since they are incapable of wanting to survive (and of other long-term desires). This view is often found in combination with the view that a baby is *not the same individual* as the 'person' who may result from that baby (we will return to this point in the next chapter).

The view that interests in some way presuppose desires, or the capacity for desires, is said to be compatible with recognizing the interests of those in temporary comas, who cannot now desire to survive, but have wanted to survive in the past. If such people survive and recover, this desire and other long-term desires will be satisfied, instead of being thwarted. This view is also said to be compatible with recognizing the interests of those who have been socially conditioned not to have certain desires: for example, slaves who have been socially conditioned not to desire their freedom. After all, not having freedom may militate against the satisfaction of other desires of the person who has been so conditioned.[7]

There is, however, a fundamental flaw, on one view of interests, in this kind of approach. To insist on a connection, of one kind or another, between interests and desires[8] is, on this view, to fail to do justice to the distinction between *having* an interest in something and *taking* an interest in something: desiring it or wanting it. This distinction can be seen in the conflict people experience between their interests and their desires. Suicidal people can have an interest in living, although they do not want to live. Alcoholics can have an interest in drying out, although they want to go on drinking. Whole networks of desires around which a person's life is structured may come to be rejected by that person for very good reasons. For example, a neo-Nazi may come to see that he does not, as he previously thought, have an interest in devoting his life to the neo-Nazi cause.

With regard to newborn babies, doctors will normally assume, in the way they treat their infant patients, that these patients have interests in benefits they do not understand or desire. For example, infants are seen as having interests in their future rational awareness. Even if a child who undergoes a certain harm – for example, mental damage due to neglect – will never come to regret that harm, it is seen as against the child's interests to let the harm occur. The view that a child can have interests only in things which he or she can now desire, or will desire in the future, is not borne out either by common sense, or by standard medical practice.

The basic human goods

Human beings have, it would appear, *objective* interests in what will truly do them good, whether or not they desire it, have desired it in the past or will desire it in the future. What kind of thing might be said to *do a human being good*, in this objective sense? This question has been asked, and answers to it proposed, over centuries of ethical reflection. In recent years, one group of writers in particular have proposed a list of 'basic human goods', among which they include the goods of life and health, knowledge and friendship (Grisez *et al.* 1987; Finnis *et al.* 1987).[9] These writers claim that the 'human goods' are simply *seen* as good by the person with sufficient experience: that they are good is not, in other words, derived from some fact more basic. Through learning and thinking and having friends, we directly see that knowledge and friendship are good: not just good instrumentally (although they often are good instrumentally) but good in themselves. Knowledge and friendship fulfil us – do us good – in the most immediate sense, as soon as we know and have friends.

To say that something would do us good is not, of course, to say that we must or may obtain it on every possible occasion. There are many cases in which we are debarred by (for example) the rights of others from seeking to obtain what is in some sense in our interest. The good of knowledge is in our interest; however, we may not increase our knowledge – for example, in the area of science – by harmful experimentation on human beings. The reason for this is precisely the human good – in this case, that of life and health – which will be damaged if we pursue our research. The good of knowledge is one which, in this situation, we will need to forgo.

The connection between the human goods and moral norms is therefore not completely straightforward. The human goods are, however, the 'building blocks' of morality, in that morality is closely concerned with what fulfils us and other people as the kind of being we are.

The good of life

The human goods are said to include the good of life in *any* condition, as well as life in a state of physical well-being. This is, of course, a much contested claim, which will be discussed in the next chapter. Here it will suffice to note that the *instrumental* value of life is hard to deny, whether or not life has *intrinsic* value. For example, life for John Pearson meant that he could later enjoy the human good of friendship (always assuming he was treated in a friendly way by others). It seems unlikely that a life in an institution (assuming he was neither adopted, nor fostered, nor brought up by his parents) would be so dreadful as to be deprived of goods such as friendship altogether. The interests of John in his future well-being, to which his life is instrumental, would thus appear to constitute one reason why it might be wrong to bring about his death.

Consequentialism

However, there is one approach to moral reasoning which has been used to defend killing[10] babies with disabilities, even if their lives are agreed to be worthwhile. This approach is *consequentialism* (also called, in its most familiar form, *utilitarianism*[11]). On this approach, what we ought morally to do is determined by what will produce the *best overall result*. According to *act consequentialism*, we should act, in every situation, so as to produce the best result. According to *rule consequentialism*, we should *follow the rule or practice* the adoption of which will produce the best result.[12] We are justified in taking any action, or adopting any practice, which will produce the greatest possible good, or the least possible bad. By 'good' and 'bad' can be meant different things: pleasure and pain, satisfied or thwarted preferences,[13] or even degrees of participation in the 'basic human goods'.

Note the difference between this approach and non-consequentialist approaches to moral reasoning. Non-consequentialists may happily accept that we should seek to obtain 'a good' (if not 'the best') result – but only within certain moral limits. According to the non-consequentialist view of *moral absolutism*, there are certain things we ought never to do, even to obtain a very good result or to prevent a very bad one (Anscombe 1958; Garcia 1993; Denyer 1997). For example, it would always be wrong to torture someone, even if this were the only way of preventing some terrible disaster.

So what would a consequentialist say about the choice to kill a baby with Down's syndrome?[14] A consequentialist of the kind who believes that we should maximize pleasant experiences might object to killing a baby with Down's on the grounds that the world would contain fewer pleasant experiences if the baby were to die. However, another consequentialist[15] might accept killing the baby on the grounds that more good would be obtained from his death than would be obtained from his life. People with Down's will often lead happy lives and bring happiness to others; however, they do have a shorter lifespan than most human beings. If one of the parents of a Down's syndrome baby refused to have another child unless the first child died, killing that child might be, for the other parent, the only way[16] of securing a state of affairs in which a child is born with a normal lifespan, thus producing more pleasure both for the child and for the parents. The 'replacement' child will not only live longer, but will be – the consequentialist might argue – more productive of parental pleasure while he or she is alive. The consequentialist might also point to the advantages to the health system if the first child dies: the money saved on the care of that child could be spent on life-saving treatments for other children or for adults.

Objections to consequentialism

Consequentialism may seem at first sight an attractively simple and practical approach to resolving our ethical dilemmas. After all, how can it not make sense to do what will bring about most good? How else are we to weigh up alternatives? Can any sane moral theory require us to do *less* good than we would do by choosing some other course of action? If a theory should make this requirement, how could it be rational to accept it?

The consequentialist approach to moral reasoning has, then, some intuitive appeal. However, it has also been the target of a wide range of objections. One such objection concerns the kind of demands consequentialism could impose. While other moral systems make heavy demands on people in some situations, consequentialism could, quite possibly, make such demands every day of our lives. In at least one form of consequentialism,[17] it is never permissible to refrain from doing what will maximize good. If killing a baby will maximize good, then I must kill a baby. If working day and night to save babies, at great cost to my own well-being, will maximize good, then I must do that. People may never please themselves, or rest from their labours, except insofar as consequentialism itself requires them to do this. (For example, consequentialism might require them to rest so as to gain strength for the next round of maximizing good.) The difference which many people see between what is morally praise-worthy and what is morally required has no place at all in this approach.[18]

In any case, this approach gives us (the critic may continue) an impossible task in asking us to compare an indefinite number of options (Denyer 1997: 54) and then choose 'the best' (or one at least as good as any other). In contrast, non-consequentialist approaches will often leave us free to choose one among many good options, providing we avoid any option which is seen as morally excluded. Moreover, even a choice between a limited number of options is impossible to make on consequentialist grounds. It is impossible, in the first place, because no-one knows what the future will hold. For example, if we save a person's life, that person may or may not go on to have children, who may or may not have children themselves. The person saved, and his or her descendants, will perform many actions, good and bad, assuming they exist in the world. The implications of saving the person's life are incalculable, in some important respects. Is it not unrealistic to require that we even attempt to calculate all the results of our possible actions, no matter how remote? If this is impossible – as it seems to be – how can consequentialism be seen as a practical guide to making moral decisions? If total results are impossible to determine, how can they guide our behaviour?

Second, such calculations are impossible (the critic may wish to add) because they involve comparing what cannot be compared. Even if we somehow knew the total results of each of a limited number of options, how is it possible to compare the different values which each of these options has to offer? Which is better, for example: total happiness for all existing and possible people? Total happiness for existing people only? Mild happiness for a large number of people or intense happiness for a smaller number of people? A large amount of knowledge for one person or a small amount of friendship for three?

A consequentialist might reply that even non-consequentialists make comparisons between different values, including values of different kinds. For example, non-consequentialists who believe in 'human goods' may accept that it is possible to give 'too much' attention to one good to the detriment of others in the life one chooses to lead. We might think of a person who devotes herself to knowledge to the total neglect of friendship and health. It may be asked why, if a non-consequentialist can compare different values for the purpose of making choices, a consequentialist cannot do the same. Even if such values cannot be *numerically* compared (one is not 1.5 times greater than the other) can they not be *ordinally* compared (one is greater, less or about the same as the other)? Admittedly, friendship, health and knowledge are goods of different kinds – but can they not be compared in terms of the relative importance of their current contribution to a person's well-being?

Agent relativity

The non-consequentialist may concede that values – including values of different kinds – can at least sometimes be compared.[19] However, there remain many serious objections to the consequentialist approach. Perhaps the most serious objection of all is that concerning *agent relativity*:[20] the importance for the agent – the person who acts – of the fact that the action will be *his*. The impact on the person who acts is, on this view, central to wrongdoing. An act such as torture immediately harms not only the victim but the perpetrator. This harm will normally include a harm to the character of the latter,[21] which is inflicted via the harm done to his or her relationship with the victim. So far the consequentialist could, perhaps, agree: a consequentialist could treat 'becoming a torturer' as something bad she wants to minimize in the world. However, the non-consequentialist goes further than this, and says that the person who acts must above all refrain from doing the kind of thing which causes, and expresses, a bad moral character.[22] Torture, as an unjust action, both causes and expresses injustice in the torturer. Even if I know that if I do not torture a prisoner, not one but two other people will take over, I must not torture the prisoner, as I am responsible first and foremost for what I do myself.[23] I am responsible for *my* relationship to the potential victim of my own injustice, in a way that I am not responsible for the relationship of others to that person.

Here we can return to the consequentialist claim that we should do what will bring about 'most good'. The non-consequentialist may agree with the consequentialist that a large amount of torture is in itself 'worse' (that is, more harmful) than a small amount of torture. What is more harmful is more to be prevented, other things being equal, than what is less harmful.[24] Other things are not, however, equal when the only way of preventing a large amount of torture (for example) is to torture someone oneself. In this case, from one's own point of view, a large amount of torture should not be seen as more to be prevented than a small amount of torture for which one will be personally responsible.

Inputs and outputs

For some, at least, who oppose consequentialism, it is the *input* of our actions, not the *output*, which determines their moral goodness or badness. By 'input' is meant the intentions, desires and concerns of the person who acts. Two actions with very different 'outputs' in terms of their impact on the world may be morally identical in terms of their 'inputs': the intentions, desires and concerns which they express (Garcia 1990, 1993). Of course, part of the 'input' is the agent's attitude to the external world, expressed in what the agent foresees and accepts as well as what she intends. However, to foresee and accept an 'output' of our choices which constitutes an unjust input *for others* – for example, their choice to torture – need not be to be unjust ourselves. In contrast, the intention to engage in torture ourselves, however benevolent our *further* intentions, expresses a lack of respect for the victim's well-being which we thereby attack. This lack of respect is not found in merely foreseeing that others will torture, as an 'output' of our own refusal to do so. In one case, harm is *intended* by us; in the other, it is merely that good is not intended, since it cannot be achieved without intending serious harm.

Moral absolutes

Those who defend the view that there are 'moral absolutes' are claiming there are choices we should *never* make; in contrast, choices we should *always* make are (to say the least) very rare. Some choices are always wrong, but other choices, which may be right in certain situations, are not always right or always required. Rescuing someone from torture, for example, would sometimes be morally praiseworthy but not morally required, in view of the dangers for the rescuer. It might even be morally wrong, if the rescuer had more urgent duties elsewhere. In contrast, *torturing* the prisoner is an example of a choice we should *never* make – a choice which is always wrong. The same could, perhaps, be said about the choice to kill an innocent human being.

We may appear to have strayed a long way from the case we began by discussing. However, it is clearly not possible to say anything very useful about a particular case without referring to the general moral principles which link that case to other cases. In the next chapter, we will begin by looking at a case of intentional killing[25] of someone whose condition was considerably more serious than Down's syndrome. We will also pursue the discussion of one way of defending the killing of non-competent patients: the defence that these patients, though living *human beings*, are not *human persons*.

Chapter 2

The unconscious patient

The Bland case

Tony Bland was a young man injured in the Hillsborough football stadium disaster of 1989. Until 1993, the year he died, he remained in what was diagnosed as being a 'persistent vegetative state' (PVS). In this condition, the patient is 'awake but not aware': able to respond to stimuli but (if the diagnosis is correct) incapable of experience. This is not coma, a sleep-like state; nor is it 'brain death', where the patient is considered to be dead.[1] In PVS the upper brain is very badly damaged; however, the brainstem is alive, maintaining functions such as breathing. Patients in PVS do not need respirators, but are normally fed by tube, since even if, in many cases, they can swallow it would take too long to feed them by spoon. The tube can be either a gastrostomy tube directly into the stomach or (as in the case of Tony Bland) a nasogastric tube through the nose into the stomach.

Airedale NHS Trust, which was caring for Tony

Bland, applied to the courts for a declaration that it would be lawful to withdraw all medical treatment – including tube-feeding – except for treatment with 'the sole purpose of enabling Anthony Bland to end his life and to die peacefully with the greatest dignity and the least distress'. Withdrawal of tube-feeding was declared to be lawful by the courts, and eventually took place. Tony Bland died some days later.

In the House of Lords, the final court of appeal, it was held that feeding could be withdrawn from a PVS patient by those with a duty of care towards that patient. Three out of five Law Lords stated that the aim of stopping feeding was to bring about Tony Bland's death. Feeding by tube was seen as a form of medical treatment which could be withdrawn if futile and therefore not in the patient's best interests. Tube-feeding Tony Bland could be regarded as futile because, in the opinion of 'a large body of informed and responsible medical opinion … existence in a vegetative state [was] regarded as not being a benefit'.

Diagnosing PVS

Since the Bland case, doubt has been cast on our ability to diagnose PVS with confidence. A number of patients formerly thought to be 'vegetative' have been enabled to communicate with others by means of a computer (Andrews *et al.* 1996). In one case, a twenty-three-year-old woman was able to communicate the fact that she wanted to live only days before a court was due to hear an application for her feeding to be withdrawn (Lightfoot and Rogers 1996). Some writers regard the whole concept of PVS with scepticism, on the grounds that there is no way of checking directly that a patient is unconscious, as opposed to uncommunicative (Borthwick 1996; Shewmon 1997: 59–60). To simplify matters, however, we will assume in the following discussion that Tony Bland was indeed unconscious, and would have remained so for the rest of his life.

Bodily persons

Tony Bland was, it would appear, alive at the time his feeding was withdrawn. Indeed, the Law Lords explicitly stated that he was alive, at least in the eyes of the medical world and the law. However, other statements by the Law Lords and lower court judges seem to suggest that Tony Bland was in some sense already dead: for example, the claim that he was 'not living a life at all' and the claim that his spirit had left the 'shell' of his body.

Clearly, Tony Bland was in a highly deprived and damaged condition. To say this is not, however, to say that Tony Bland was not a living human person. A human person is not a purely spiritual being, as an angel or a ghost might be said to be a purely spiritual being.[2] Rather, a human person is a *bodily* being – a living human 'whole' or organism. It is (so most of us believe) the *human person* who thinks, speaks, breathes and sleeps, not separate individuals only some of whom survive when certain functions are destroyed. Nor do we think that when a person's brain is damaged a new individual comes into being to take over the functions which remain. Rather, we make the natural assumption that breathing and sleeping in the brain-damaged patient are maintained by the same person – the same bodily being – who has always maintained them.

Our tendency to think that a person can survive this kind of damage can be seen from the following example. Let us imagine that a new technique for treating PVS was developed during Tony Bland's lifetime. This technique leaves the patient with total amnesia, but able to learn, as a newborn child is able to learn. Would the operation have created a new person or would it have treated an existing person – in this case, Tony Bland? It would appear that the patient who woke up after the operation would have been Tony Bland – the same individual who suffered brain damage and lay for years in an unconscious state. His *personality* would, of course, be different from what it was before he was injured, but he would be the same *person* nonetheless – the same human individual. For example, it would be a misfortune for him that he had lost the memories of his former life – which it would not be if this life were that of someone else entirely. In the same way, it would be fortunate for him that he was able to have the operation instead of being left in PVS. Tony Bland, as a living human person, would survive the operation on his brain, and would neither be joined nor replaced by a separate human individual.[3]

The concept of 'human person'

Here it may be objected that the term 'human person' refers not simply to a human individual but to a human individual *with human moral status*. It is, indeed, the case that 'human person' – a term which can be used in very different ways – is often used with moral, as well as descriptive significance. It is also the case that whereas some would say that human beings are *equal* in their basic moral status, many would say that they are not.

Many writers on ethics, in particular, would distinguish between *human beings* and *human persons*, on the grounds that not all human beings have the rights and interests of human persons. Even those who accept that human persons are *bodily* beings may want to say that only those bodily beings with highly developed mental abilities are persons with personal moral status. Since PVS patients, infants and others do not have highly developed mental abilities, they do not have the status of human persons. In support of this position, it is often claimed that persons are those who can have morally significant interests in (for example) survival, and that in order to have such interests one must have, or be able to have in the short-term future, certain desires.

We will be looking further at this position in Chapter 4. As we saw in Chapter 1, there is a problem with tying interests to the desires of those who have them, in that people would appear to *have* interests in things in which they cannot *take* an interest. Tony Bland, for example, had an interest in – in that he would have benefited from – a cure of his condition, even if none was available at the time. Tony Bland also had an interest in not being treated with disrespect by those around him: for example, in not being made the butt of unkind jokes at his expense. Indeed, Tony Bland had interests in all the various aspects of human fulfilment, despite the fact that many of these aspects were unavailable to him – and in any case, undesired by him – in his damaged state. Tony Bland was, like us, a human being, whose fulfilment consisted in what fulfils any human being. Tony Bland's interest in health, for example, remained the same throughout his life; it did not disappear after a certain number of months in a state of unconsciousness. At any time during his life, Tony Bland had interests in health and in other forms of flourishing appropriate to the kind of being to which he belonged. Since he belonged to the *human* kind of being, and had interests in what fulfils a member of that (rational) kind of being, it seems wrong to try to place him in a separate moral class from our own.

The good of life

However, even if Tony Bland *was* a human 'person', in the same moral class as our own, questions can still be asked about what his interests were after he failed to recover. Tony Bland had an interest in recovery; did he also have an interest in survival in a persistent vegetative state? Or were the judges right to accept what they saw as the view of 'a responsible body of medical opinion': the view that life in PVS is of no value whatsoever?

In the previous chapter, life was included in a list of so-called 'human goods'. On one theory, our knowledge of human goods – basic aspects of human fulfilment – is not derived from other things we know. It is not possible, on this view, to 'prove' (in the sense of derive from something else) that life is good for human beings, any more than we can 'prove' that knowledge or friendship, for example, is good for human beings. What is good for human beings must be directly seen (or not, as the case may be).[4]

However, to say that life is *not* good for human beings in certain situations is to take a position with disturbing implications. To say this is, in most cases,[5] to say that it is either bad in itself or a matter of indifference that some human beings exist in the world. Is such a position compatible with respect for those human beings? What if we were to use PVS patients to practise amputations? What if we were to use them in trials for developing car safety? Given that human beings are human *organisms* – that is, self-organizing bodily wholes – is it not in their interests to continue their vital functions, even in a highly damaged state? Just as the organism is harmed, from the point of view of health, by being deprived of *some* of its functions, is it not supremely harmed, from this point of view, by being deprived of *all* of its functions?[6]

Respect for life

It may be objected that if we accept that life is good in itself, we will have to accept that we should go to all possible lengths to support it. Whatever Tony Bland needed – whether tube-feeding, a respirator or even a heart transplant – would have had to be provided in the interests of sustaining a valuable life. Yet it would surely be a gross misuse of resources[7] if a heart transplant, for example, was given to a patient who could never regain consciousness.

However, such 'heroic' treatment is not normally proposed by those who hold that life is good in itself. A distinction is normally recognized between the *positive* demands and the *negative* demands of the good of life. The good of life must compete with other goods, and with life in other patients, when it comes to allocating resources. There is no positive demand that we go to all possible lengths to promote the good of life – or indeed, any other human good. In contrast, there is a *negative* demand that we do not *choose to end* a human life, at least in the case of an innocent human being. It is possible, as we have seen, to choose to end a life by omission. However, we need not be choosing to end a patient's life if we give resources to those who can benefit more, even if we foresee that the patient not treated will die sooner as a result.

The goal of medicine

There is another consideration which might lead us to limit life-supporting measures for a patient: the proper goal or purpose of medicine. Some ethicists argue that medicine and nursing care have separate, though complementary, goals. While the goal of nursing is, among other things, to sustain the patient's life, the goal of medicine is to promote health, or some approximation to health, or failing that, to palliate the symptoms of disease (Gormally 1994: 134–5, 138–9). An approximation to health, on this theory, must include the potential for some degree of awareness, so that if a patient is permanently unconscious, treatment is futile in relation to the special goals of medicine. Treatment may not, of course, be *altogether* futile, in that it may sustain the patient's life, but will be *medically* futile if sustaining life is not the goal of medicine.

A doctor who took such a view might withhold life-saving treatment from a PVS patient, not with the aim of shortening life but simply on the grounds that it would serve no medical purpose (taking a narrow definition of 'medical purpose') for the patient concerned. Even if the patient died sooner than he otherwise would as a result of not being given the treatment, this need not be the intention of the doctor in deciding – whether rightly or wrongly – that it would not be given. Of course, it *could* be the intention, and *would*, no doubt, be the intention in some cases; however, it need not be the intention.

Tube-feeding: medical treatment?

We will be returning in the next chapter to the question of side-effects of medical decisions. Is there any foundation to the claim that sustaining life is not the proper goal of medicine? It is difficult to draw a sharp line between medical and nursing interventions. However, many people do have the intuition that the more 'artificial' some life-sustaining measure – the more bodily functions it replaces and the more technology it requires[8] – the more benefit we need to expect from that measure in terms of health or some approximation to it. In other words, if there is a spectrum of cases between, on the one side, high-technology medicine and, on the other, basic nursing care, where some life-sustaining measure falls clearly on the 'technological' side of the spectrum, it must help us achieve higher goals[9] than those of basic nursing care.

In the case of PVS patients, can feeding by tube be regarded as a form – albeit a simple form – of medical treatment? Some would say yes, as the tube is substituting for bodily functions which have failed. Just as dialysis substitutes for the kidney function, and a respirator substitutes (or partially substitutes) for the function of the lungs, so feeding by tube substitutes for taking food by hand and swallowing.

It is true that some – though by no means all – PVS patients are unable to swallow. However, the fact that a function is supplied for does not always mean that to supply for it is medical treatment as opposed to nursing care. After all, nurses often substitute for functions of those who can no longer perform them. Spoonfeeding, for example, substitutes for the patient feeding him or herself. Unlike breathing, which is not normally assisted except in a medical context, nutrition is frequently assisted to some extent by those without any form of medical expertise. Young children are quite routinely spoonfed, as are sick and frail people of all ages. It is far from clear that replacing self-feeding alone (spoonfeeding) is basic nursing care, while replacing self-feeding-and-swallowing (though not digestion) falls in the category of medical treatment, and must serve a different goal.[10]

Moreover, as we have seen, diagnosis of PVS may be, in practice, far from certain. If this is the case, we run the risk, if food and fluids are withdrawn, of causing a sentient patient, for whom not merely nursing but medical treatment would be appropriate, to die painfully of thirst. If there is doubt both over the diagnosis of PVS and over the status of tube-feeding as medical treatment – and, indeed, over the proper end of medicine in its more simple forms – the safest course of action would appear to be to go on feeding by tube.

Social significance of tube-feeding

Finally, the social significance of feeding should not be overlooked. Feeding is, or can be, an expression of solidarity with the person who is being fed. To continue feeding a brain-damaged patient is one way of showing that that patient is valued: valued not for what he can do but for what he is – a fellow human being. Such an attitude is, it can be argued, valuable both to the carers[11] and to society at large. It is good for carers to value those for whom they care; it is good for all of us to live in a society where even the most deprived and damaged human beings are seen as having value.

In contrast, a decision *not* to tube-feed a brain-damaged patient may be an expression of a view which sees the patient's life as having literally no value. Such a decision may, indeed, be an expression not merely of a view which sees the patient's life as worthless, but of the intention to bring it to a close. This intention, and the view which underlies it, are, again, of great social significance: a significance which goes beyond our view of human life to our view of human beings in general. Psychologically, if not theoretically, it is a small step from saying that some human lives have no value to saying that some human beings are not in any way morally important. While this step on the part of society may not seem a problem to those who themselves believe that some human beings have no moral importance, it will be less welcome to those who believe – whatever their views on the value of life – that all human beings have moral importance, to which others have a duty to respond. Those who accept this may regard tube-feeding as at very least a form of recognition that PVS patients, despite their disability, are human moral subjects like ourselves.

Non-voluntary euthanasia

Whether feeding by tube is medical treatment, and whether patients in PVS should be tube-fed, are separate questions from the question whether feeding should be withdrawn *with the aim of causing death*. If this is the aim, as it was said to be in the Bland case, withdrawal of feeding must be discussed as what it is: a case of euthanasia by omission. As such, it must be judged in relation to the status of the patient killed, the truth of the claim that his life is not worthwhile, the truth of the claim that innocent people may not be deliberately killed, and the predicted impact on other people of bringing about their deaths. For those who assume that the patient does not have human status and/or does not have a valuable life, euthanasia may appear justified, providing (which would have to be shown) that other people are not harmed. For those who assume, on the contrary, that the patient *does* have human status *and* a life of intrinsic value, euthanasia may be seen as harming both the patient and, in the first place, those who bring about his death. On this view, the patient's life may not be attacked, even for the sake of other values. The aim is not (as it is in consequentialism) to 'maximize' life or other goods, but rather, to respect them.

Like the Arthur case, the Bland case involved a patient unable to consent to his death, and was therefore a case of *non-voluntary* euthanasia. We will now look at a case of *voluntary* euthanasia (in this case, *active* euthanasia) of a patient who was able to communicate her wish to die.

Chapter 3

The competent patient

The Cox case

Lillian Boyes, a seventy-year-old woman, had suffered for twenty years from rheumatoid arthritis. In 1991, she was dying in great pain in the Royal Hampshire County Hospital. She had ulcers on her arms and legs, vertebral fractures, swollen joints and severe limb deformity. It was agony for her to be touched, and her pain was not responding to increasing doses of diamorphine. In this dreadful medical condition, Mrs Boyes expressed a wish to die. Her doctor, Nigel Cox, who had treated her for thirteen years, told her that he could not give her active euthanasia, but agreed to withdraw all life-prolonging treatment. Following this, the pain became still worse, and Mrs Boyes asked again to be killed. After a further attempt at palliation, Dr Cox eventually gave Mrs Boyes a lethal injection of potassium chloride, a drug which has no pain-relieving properties.

Mrs Boyes' remains had already been cremated by the time Dr Cox's action was reported to the police. Dr

Cox was therefore charged with attempted murder, due to lack of evidence that he had caused Mrs Boyes' death. He was convicted by the jury, and given a twelve-month suspended prison sentence. Dr Cox was admonished by the General Medical Council, but was not struck off the register or suspended from medical practice. He was eventually reinstated by the Wessex Regional Health Authority, on condition that he went on a course in palliative care, and that he worked under supervision.

Justified homicide?

At first sight, the Cox case may appear to many a paradigm case of justified homicide. Euthanasia had been requested several times by Mrs Boyes, who was supported in her request by her sons (Singer 1994: 140). Assuming that Mrs Boyes, despite her pain, was competent to choose, this was *voluntary* euthanasia. Moreover, the patient was in great pain in the last days of her life. The case appears to test to the limit the view that the existence of a human being is in itself good.

Was there anything else which Dr Cox could and should have done? Dr Cox was, in fact, criticized strongly by specialists in palliative care for failing to refer Mrs Boyes for pain control. It was pointed out that a doctor who is unable to control a patient's pain has a duty to refer her to those better qualified to do so. Pain can, in fact, be readily controlled, in the great majority of cases, by those with expertise in this area (Twycross 1994: 2–5). In those rare cases where pain is intractable (or, at least, difficult to treat) there is always the option of sedation to the point of total unconsciousness (Twycross 1994: 563). Even if a patient has to be kept sedated until she dies, and even if the patient dies sooner than she otherwise would as a result of the sedation, sedation may still be a justified solution if other treatments fail. Sedation does not, moreover, amount to euthanasia, since in the case of euthanasia it is death, not sleep, which is sought. Sleep and death are different physical states, and to intend the one is not to intend the other, even if the other will or may be hastened as a result.

We will return to this question later in the chapter when we look at the 'principle of double effect'. Here it may be objected that the option of sedation was perhaps beside the point. After all, Mrs Boyes asked to be killed, and might have preferred this option to sedation, even if she had been given the choice. Why try to deal with her pain by sedation – certainly a fairly drastic form of treatment – rather than satisfy her wish to die? Should we not respect a patient's autonomy? Even if we grant that good palliative care should be made available to all who could benefit, what if a patient prefers euthanasia?

Worthless life?

Euthanasia – that is, *voluntary* euthanasia – is certainly often defended in terms of patient autonomy. However, it involves, on closer inspection, more than a simple response to a patient's request. Unless euthanasia is made available to all who ask for it, whatever their condition, the doctor will have to make his or her own judgement on the worthwhileness of the patient's life. Doctors are not, after all, mere machines for carrying out the wishes of their patients, but professional people with some responsibility for evaluating what they are asked to do. A doctor who supports euthanasia will therefore distinguish between those he or she thinks are *right* to want to die, because their lives are not worth living, and those he or she thinks are *wrong* to want to die, because their lives *are* worth living, though they may be (for example) temporarily depressed. While the doctor may defend euthanasia in terms of autonomy, he or she in fact believes that only *some* individuals – namely, those whose lives are not worth living – have a right to exercise their autonomy by choosing to be killed.

We are thus faced once again with the question of whether human life can have no value. Can it be true of any human being that it is better, in her state of health, that she cease to exist as a living human being? If this is not clearly true of any patient, can we act on the *assumption* it is true in the case of some patients? If we do so act, how should our action be regarded by society? If I am accused of killing another human being, should I be able to defend myself by saying not (for example) 'it was self-defence', but 'that person's life *had no value*'? What kind of effect will this have on society's view of homicide in general – and on society's view of those who are sick or disabled?

It is worth noting that if life can be literally worthless, the patient's request may not be necessary for euthanasia to be morally permissible.[1] If death is a benefit, or, at least, no harm, why should a non-competent patient be denied it, simply because he or she is unable to ask for it?[2] Why should infants, for example, or those with Alzheimer's, be denied euthanasia? Indeed, if life really has no value, why should it not be ended solely for the sake of the patient's relatives – or, for that matter, for the good of society at large?

Autonomy cannot, then, be invoked – at least in any simple fashion – in defence of euthanasia. If euthanasia *is* justifiable in some cases, the patient's request will be neither a sufficient nor, perhaps, a necessary requirement. If, on the other hand, euthanasia is *not* justifiable in *any* case, because no human life is worthless, the patient's request for euthanasia will not be in any way persuasive. A request for euthanasia will need to be treated like any other request for a harmful procedure (Oderberg 1997: 234–5, 239) – for example, cutting off a healthy limb. Rather than acceding to the patient's request to be killed, the doctor, on this view, should offer, or arrange for, pain relief, counselling and other forms of medical and social support.[3] A doctor should not, in other words, agree with a patient, however distressed or despairing, that her life is not worthwhile.

Patient autonomy

A doctor who refuses requests for euthanasia need not refuse to recognize the role of patient autonomy in other situations. There are, on the contrary, many situations where the doctor may and should abide by what the patient decides. The right of the patient to refuse medical treatment is sometimes presented as a twentieth-century discovery; however, there is a centuries-old tradition according to which the doctor is only entitled to treat the competent patient with his or her consent.[4] The question traditionally asked by moral theologians – the medical ethicists of their day – was not so much what the *doctor's* duties were with regard to the preservation of life, but what were the duties of the *patient*. Since it was assumed that competent patients *did* have certain duties to look after their own lives and health, the question was under what circumstances patients could consider themselves excused from this or that treatment or procedure.

The question arises, of course, with equal force today. Competent adults have some responsibility – indeed, the primary responsibility – for their own well-being. If life and health is an aspect of human well-being – a 'basic human good' – then it is possible to fail in respect for one's own participation in this good. The heavy drinker or smoker, for example, may be wrongfully accepting harm to life and health. In the same way, the person who puts off consulting a doctor for fear of hearing unpleasant news may be acting wrongly – however understandably – with regard to life and health.

'Ordinary' and 'extraordinary' means[5]

What, then, are our duties as patients, or potential patients, with regard to the preservation of life? What are the corresponding duties of doctors and other health professionals? Answers to these questions are often phrased in terms of a contrast between what are called 'ordinary' and 'extraordinary' means or measures of prolonging life. It should be noted that the terms 'ordinary' and 'extraordinary' can be used in different ways. As used by doctors, 'ordinary' and 'extraordinary' will often mean 'standard' or 'non-standard'. As used by ethicists, the term 'ordinary' is often used to describe those means of prolonging life which are *morally required* in view of the duty (of the doctor and/or patient) to preserve life and health. In contrast, the term 'extraordinary' is used to describe those means or measures which are *not* in this way morally required. A treatment which is standard for a certain class of patient may be more *likely* to be morally 'ordinary' (that is, morally required) than a treatment which is non-standard. However, there may well be reasons why the standard treatment is not morally required in the case of an individual patient.

Once again, it is useful at this point to think about human fulfilment in general. The good of life and health is (so the theory runs) only one of the 'basic human goods' in which we can participate. Participation in other goods – for example, knowledge – can limit the extent to which we make ourselves as healthy as we might be. Moreover, we may have special commitments which are simply incompatible with a very healthy lifestyle. For example, parents may find they have to let their own health slide to some extent in the course of caring for their children.[6]

Even in the absence of special commitments, however, there is no obligation for a patient to take measures to promote life and health if these measures will involve excessive burdens. Here we might think of the pain or discomfort which can accompany medical treatments, or of the financial cost of treatments to the patient, family, hospital or health service. We might also think of those burdens to the patient which vary greatly from one individual to another: for example, the patient's fear or repugnance at the prospect of losing a limb through amputation.[7]

A treatment or life-sustaining measure can be extraordinary because it is too painful, frightening, hazardous or disruptive for the patient, or because it is financially too burdensome to the patient, family, hospital or health service. A treatment can also be too burdensome in other ways to those who are caring for the patient – for example, it can take up time or use facilities which are urgently needed by patients who would benefit more.[8]

A treatment can also be extraordinary because it is simply futile. For example, those who are dying of one illness have no obligation to accept treatment for a second life-threatening condition which is at a less advanced stage.[9] Often, however, a treatment will be extraordinary not because that treatment will be altogether futile, but because its burdens will be disproportionate to the benefits it will bring.

For example, resuscitation of a terminal patient may impose burdens which, though not great, are excessive in relation to the slight prolongation of life it may achieve. The aim in deciding not to resuscitate may not be to shorten the life of such a patient, but merely to withhold a treatment which is thought to promise insufficient benefit. Sometimes, of course, it is not at all easy to determine the burdens and benefits of possible treatments. If the patient in question is competent, it is appropriate to consult him or her with regard to such 'borderline' treatments, so that the patient can weigh up the burdens and benefits him or herself. While a doctor should not be expected to carry out treatments which are clearly unwarranted, the help of the competent patient will be needed in evaluating borderline cases.

Duties of doctors and nurses

When it comes to accepting a treatment which is offered, the patient has rights and obligations. In the light of these rights and obligations, doctors and nurses should encourage the patient to accept those treatments which they believe are reasonable in the circumstances, while bearing in mind the fact that the burdens of treatment for the patient will vary from person to person, and that in any case it is the patient's responsibility to accept or decline treatments.[10] Normally the only case in which the doctor or nurse could be entitled to override the patient's refusal would be if the patient did not appear to be truly competent at the time of refusing treatment, and/or if the patient's motive for refusing it was suicidal. Thus, for example, a rescued suicide victim who refused to have his or her stomach pumped out would call for a different response from a non-suicidal patient who refused some treatment because it was very unpleasant.

Suicidal refusals of treatment

It is difficult to argue that suicidal people may be protected from self-harm in the form of a 'positive act', but may not be protected from self-harm in the form of an omission with exactly the same motivation. It is also difficult to argue that those who are physically ill and suicidal should be treated in a radically different way from those who are physically well and suicidal. Unless we are to acknowledge publicly that those with certain conditions have lives of no value, we should offer the physically ill and suicidal, within the limits of our resources, the same kind of protection we offer the physically well and suicidal. After all, suicidal feelings are not a necessary concomitant of any physical disorder. The ill and suicidal may value their lives very differently if given an adequate level of support.

It is important here to remember the *social dimension* of suicide – and, in particular, the social dimension of suicide which is assisted or tolerated by care-givers. Such assistance or toleration can be expected to have a demoralizing effect on the ill and disabled generally, and on society at large. It will be seen as a public statement of the worthlessness of life with some conditions – or at least, as a statement that (in contrast to the case of other suicidal people) no-one cared enough to intervene in the case of those with such conditions. Rather than looking for ways to improve the lot of the ill and suicidal, society will see suicide as an 'easy way out', both for patients themselves and – perhaps even more – for other people. A positive climate of medical care, in which carers seek actively to ameliorate the lot of those who are suffering, will be hard to combine with a fatalistic and/or collusive approach to patient suicide.

Both for the sake of the suicidal themselves, and for the sake of other sick people and society at large, suicidal refusals of treatment should not be seen as inviolable. Intervention, whether in treating the patient, or in referring him or her for psychiatric help will, in contrast, be appropriate.

However, it should not be assumed that patients are suicidal merely on the basis of their refusal of some life-prolonging treatment. The fact that a patient foresees an earlier death as a result of refusing such treatment in no way proves that an earlier death is his or her aim in refusing. Rather, the patient may simply be exercising his or her right to determine what treatments are appropriate, in view of the benefits and burdens those treatments are expected to bring.

Non-competent patients

In the case of *non-competent* patients, of course, it is competent adults who must decide what treatments are appropriate in view of their benefits and burdens. For example, if a baby is born premature, the paediatrician must make a judgement on the extent to which intensive care is likely to benefit that baby, and on the burdens it is likely to bring. In making this judgement, the paediatrician will need to look at what is sometimes called the baby's 'quality of life', both during the period in intensive care, and after, if the baby survives.

'Quality of life'

Are we, then, back with the question of judging if the patient's life will be worthwhile? We need to distinguish here between two very different views of life which the term 'quality of life' can be used to describe. According to the first view, the patient's life in certain conditions has *no* 'quality' or value (and should, perhaps, be brought to a close). Whatever is thought to give a life value – perhaps some form of positive mental experience – will be altogether lacking in some patients. According to the second view, in contrast, the patient's life will *always* have some objective value, even if it does not always have *enough* value to justify certain interventions. 'Quality of life' is used, in this context, to refer to the value of the patient's 'well-being', while acknowledging the value of his or her 'being' or existing *per se*.

Health is an aspect of the good of life: human bodily existence.[11] Human beings are less fulfilled, from the point of view of this particular good, the less healthy they are. This is not to say that human beings are less *morally important* the less healthy they are. On the contrary, it is precisely *because* they and their interests are morally important that these interests – including that in life and health – should be taken seriously by doctors. Doctors should not be too pessimistic in assessing the degree to which a treatment can benefit a patient. However, when there really is no (or little) chance of bene-fiting the patient to any great extent, the interest of the patient in being spared the burdens of the treatment should be given due weight.

To say that a treatment will not benefit a patient sufficiently to justify its burdens is not to say that the patient's life will have no value during the treatment, or after it is given. The *fundamental*, 'core' value of the patient's life can still be seen as intrinsic to that life, such that it is always good in itself, not bad in itself, that the patient continue to exist. However, the only *absolute* implication of this value which can be reasonably claimed is the *negative* duty not to *choose to end* the life of an innocent human being. With regard to *supporting* life, where the intention is not to end it, by act or by omission, we will have less and less reason to do this the more and more burdensome the means of support, and the fewer goods can be obtained for the patient over and above the good of life. It is, in short, permissible to consider a patient's 'quality of life' leading up to, during and after treatment in determining whether treatment is worthwhile in relation to the burdens it imposes. It is *not* permissible to assume that life in a certain condition has *no* 'quality' or value, and may, for that reason, be deliberately curtailed.

To return to the case of a competent patient's refusal of medical treatment, refusal because of some negative aspect of the treatment (the loss of a limb, for example) need not involve either the intention to die or the assumption that life in a certain condition would be worthless. Rather, life with some undesired aspect is rejected, not in favour of death but in favour of life (albeit a shorter life) *without* that undesired aspect. The patient would prefer to live a shorter time with two legs than a longer time with one. Such a person is rather like someone who chooses to live in a country with primitive medical facilities. The person who chooses to live in this country may foresee that he will or may die sooner than he would otherwise have died. Nonetheless, he is not *choosing death* simply by choosing to live in the country he happens to prefer. The same can be said of the patient who refuses some treatment he finds unappealing, while foreseeing and accepting that his life will be shortened as a result. As we have seen, such a refusal will not always be *justified* on the patient's part; however, it will not be suicidal.

Principle of double effect

What is the basis for the idea that death – one's own or a patient's – may be accepted, at least in some cases, but may not be intended? As we saw in Chapters 1 and 2, to recognize something as good – in this case, human life – is not to say that this good must be pursued on every possible occasion. Every time we pursue one good option, we cut off chances of pursuing other, incompatible good options. We cannot simultaneously save lives, see our friends, spend time with our families and engage in pure research. It would clearly be absurd to blame ourselves for all the good things we did not do, simply because we were doing other good things. It must, then, be permissible, often, if not always, to accept the bad effects of a choice to do something good.

A moral principle which deals with the acceptance of bad effects of what we choose to do is the so-called *principle of double effect*.[12] According to this principle, it can make a difference morally whether we *intend*, as an end or means, the bad results of our behaviour or merely *foresee and accept* them as a side-effect of choosing something else. Thus if I am a doctor at the scene of an accident, I may decide to treat one victim rather than another, not with the aim of making one die, but simply because I cannot treat both, and the one I do treat has a better chance of survival. Or if I am a doctor who is constantly in demand for doing life-saving operations, I am not guilty of the death of innocent people simply because I do not spend all my waking hours doing life-saving operations. For one thing, I may have duties to my family; for another, to spend my waking hours doing operations would be beyond what is morally required even of someone committed to saving lives in her line of work.[13] But in any case, whatever my responsibilities as a doctor, I will not be guilty of *intentional killing* if I do not *intend* that people die as an outcome of my choices, but merely *foresee* that they will die as an outcome of my choices. I may be intending *not to treat some people*; however, I am not intending not to treat these people *in order that they die*.

Acts and omissions

It should be stressed that the distinction between what we *intend* in choosing and what we *accept* in choosing crosses the divide between positive acts and omissions. Both omissions and positive acts may result in people dying who need not have died, where our intention is not to cause these deaths, but to accomplish something else. For example, I build a bridge, on which, eventually, over the years, some motorists will be killed. Or I prescribe a drug, to which, eventually, over the years, some patients will have fatal reactions. In neither case is it my intention that people die – whether by driving off my bridge or by collapsing after a dose of my drug. My actions are therefore different from the actions of, for example, building my bridge with the aim of killing motorists, or prescribing my drug, not to treat patients, but to discover the fatal dose.

A more familiar application of the principle of double effect is the case mentioned earlier where a terminal patient is given palliative drugs which will or may shorten her life. It is generally accepted among those who work in palliative care that to give drugs with the sole intention of relieving pain is not euthanasia. The shortening of life is a side-effect like any other: foreseen (at least in some cases)[14] but not for that reason intended. The intention with which the drugs are given – that of relieving pain, not shortening life[15] – makes giving them, not an act of euthanasia, but an act of palliative care.

In the same way for omissions, it is the *intention with which* life-sustaining measures are omitted which makes the omission the kind of behaviour it is. For example, if a nurse omits to feed a patient because he is very close to death and feeding would be unduly burdensome to him, the nurse's choice is not euthanasia. If, on the other hand, she omits to feed the patient because she thinks the patient's life is worthless and wants that life to end, her choice *is* euthanasia by omission, as her intention is to hasten death. If it is wrong to assume a life is worthless and to end it on those grounds, it is wrong whether we choose to end it by acting, or by refraining from action. While 'letting a patient die' is not euthanasia if the aim is not to hasten death, if the aim *is* to hasten death it is euthanasia, no less than giving the patient a lethal injection.

What is meant by 'aim' here is not simply the *motive* – that is, the *longer-term* intention – but what we choose to do with that motive in mind. The nurse who kills a patient may have a compassionate motive – that of ending suffering – but she also has the intention to kill. As was argued in Chapter 1, for an act to be morally justified, *all* the intentions involved in that act must be morally justified, not simply the longer-term intentions. If just one intention – the intention to end a patient's life – is morally wrong in itself, this is enough to make the nurse's action morally wrong, however 'well-meaning' or well-motivated it is.

Lethal bodily invasions

Even if the nurse's aim were not to kill the patient, but simply to inject him, on the doctor's orders, with a substance she knew would do the patient no good, but only lethal harm, this intention would in itself suffice to make her action morally wrong. In the same way, if the doctor stood by with the intention that the patient's body be invaded in this way, the doctor would also be wrongfully choosing a bodily invasion of a kind which can only do harm. It is not only death which must not be chosen by the doctor or nurse, but bodily invasions which are foreseen to do harm, and only harm, to the subject – as where human beings are used in lethal experiments. Even if a Nazi doctor did not care if his victims lived or died, but simply intended to assess the short-term effects on their bodies of certain drugs, the doctor's intention to invade their bodies in a way he knew would do no good, but only lethal harm, would be enough to identify what he is doing as a grossly immoral course of action.

When dealing with the principle of double effect, we should remember that death is not the only thing which may not be intended for an innocent human being.[16] The Nazi doctor is not 'let off the hook' simply because he can sincerely say that he is not intending the death of his victims. What he *is* intending – non-therapeutic bodily invasion of a kind he knows will be lethal – is quite enough to categorize his behaviour as very wrong indeed. Admittedly, death itself is not his intention; however, death will undoubtedly be caused by something which *is* his intention: non-therapeutic bodily invasion. The doctor has no right to carry out such a bodily invasion, or to accept the lethal side-effects of so doing. Nor will it avail him to point to the lives which may be saved in the future as a result of his experiments: a good effect he says will 'outweigh' the lethal side-effects of what he is intending here and now. His behaviour is already ruled out by an absolute moral prohibition, which takes no account of such good effects for those other than the victim. It is only when *none* of a person's intentions are *already* morally prohibited – in themselves and/or because of the side-effects with which they are immediately connected – that it is appropriate to take such good effects into account.

Accepting side-effects

A doctor or nurse who intends either the death of a patient (or some other innocent human being) or a bodily invasion of a kind foreseen to do him or her only serious harm[17] is *always* doing wrong, unlike the doctor or nurse who accepts some harm to a patient as an unintended side-effect of beneficial treatment. To say that harm to a patient is not intended but only accepted, and that the intention is to benefit the patient, is not, however, the end of the story. Sometimes accepting a side-effect is reasonable; other times it is not. We are morally responsible not merely for our intentions in acting, but for the foreseen side-effects of our actions, which need to be proportionate to the good we hope to achieve. Indeed, we are responsible not merely for the side-effects we *did* foresee, but also (in a somewhat different way) for those we ought to have foreseen, and did not. It should also be noted that there will be some cases in which causing harm as a side-effect is just as wrong as causing it on purpose. For example, if a doctor omits to treat a patient, not with the aim of causing death but with the aim of stealing the drugs and selling them on the black market, his or her action may be morally no better than omitting to treat with the aim of causing death.

Despite this, it can still be argued that the difference between effects we intend and those we merely foresee is sometimes the difference between what is morally justified and what is unjustified behaviour. Every choice we make has some negative side-effects – if only because we are not making some other, incompatible choice which would have done good in some other way. I mentioned earlier the case of the doctor at the scene of the accident who lets one victim die while she is treating another. It would be patently unreasonable to *blame* the doctor for the death of victim B while she was treating victim A, in the way we *would* blame the doctor if she deliberately killed victim B, or brought about his death by omission of treatment, so she could give his organs to victim A.

Moral integrity

Some would say that these distinctions are artificial, and that we should simply act in such a way as to obtain the best result. If taking the organs would obtain the best result – either in one case or as standard procedure – then this is what we ought to do. This approach, it will be remembered from the first chapter, is that of *consequentialism*, which holds that an act or practice may be judged right and wrong only in relation to its overall results.

However, as was argued in the first chapter, what makes an action right or wrong is not simply the consequences of acting on the external world. People are, indeed, responsible, at least in some degree, for producing good results in the external world; however, they are responsible, above all, for *not* doing (in the sense of not intending) certain kinds of harm. In making immoral choices of this kind, our characters will normally be affected.[18] Taking the organs from a patient who is killed or 'let die' for the purpose might well have good results for the recipients of those organs. However, such results are too dearly purchased by the choice to kill an innocent human being: a choice which will have a profoundly harmful effect not only on the human being killed but on those who choose to bring about his death.

Good character or 'virtue' is, on this approach to morality, both instrumental to, and an aspect of, human fulfilment.[19] The doctor who fails in relation to the virtue of justice, by treating a patient as a mere source of transplant material, has harmed him or herself in the process. In view of the harm done to his or her character, such a doctor's commitment to patients in the future has been undermined. He or she is more likely to treat this commitment in the future as something contingent: something which may be overridden whenever the 'greater good' is thought to require it. However, even if no such temptation presents itself at any time in the future, the doctor's character – an aspect of his or her well-being – has been changed for the worse.

By making choices, we make ourselves, for good or bad, people of one kind rather than another. Some choices help to make us good human beings, while other choices have the reverse effect on the kind of people we become. This can be seen in our more mundane choices, as well as in those choices which involve a question of life and death. For example, doctors who are unpleasant to their patients – rude, careless and unsympathetic – are making themselves unpleasant human beings, who are likely to be unpleasant in the future. In contrast, doctors who are considerate with their patients are making themselves considerate human beings, who are likely to be considerate in the future. In acting well, we strengthen our dispositions to be (for example) considerate, fair and generous in our dealings with others.

Of course, what *counts* as being fair or considerate will often vary according to situations. It is only a very few actions which are always wrong, whatever the situation. However, it is important to bear in mind that morality is not, in any straightforward sense, about 'getting good results'. Morality is rather about what we choose, for ourselves and for others, and about how what we choose affects the 'contents of the heart'.[20] To will the death of a patient, as an end or means, is likely to have a worse impact on us – quite apart from any impact on the patient – than to accept the death of a patient in the course of willing something else. Having said this, it is certainly possible to tolerate a bad side-effect unfairly: this too will have a harmful impact not only on the people we mistreat but on the people we ourselves become.

Chapter 4

Abortion

At the start of this book, we looked at the role of emotion in our responses to moral problems. Abortion is a subject which tends to evoke particularly powerful emotional reactions. Many women have had an abortion themselves at some time in their lives. Many men and women have been involved in an abortion in some other way. The subject can arouse strong emotions in those who have themselves been involved in an abortion. It can also arouse strong emotions in those (the groups can overlap) who wish to protect what they believe to be a child.

Justification and culpability

In approaching the question of abortion, it is worth making one point very clear. Our interest here is in the rights and wrongs of abortion, not the good or bad faith of those who have, perform or recommend abortions. Here as elsewhere, the question of culpability is a

separate question from the question of whether or not a certain choice is morally justified. It is possible to do something wrong while believing one is doing something right. It is also possible to do what one knows or believes to be wrong under serious emotional pressure: a pressure which will lessen the degree of culpability one has for doing what one does.

Is abortion the kind of choice which – leaving aside the question of culpability – is morally unjustified? Many would say that abortion is, on the contrary, justified in most or all cases. For example, many feminists would argue that a woman has the right to decide what happens 'in and to' her body. Some feminist writers maintain that even if (which they would deny) the foetus is a human moral subject, the fact that it is physically dependent on the pregnant woman means that the woman has the right to determine whether or not the pregnancy continues.[1] Feminists who defend abortion[2] will sometimes argue further that women have abortions out of respect for motherhood: because they are unable to meet the demands of motherhood, and therefore do not wish to give birth.

Bodily dependence

How should we evaluate the claim that a woman may choose abortion whatever the status of the foetus? Pregnancy is not, we need to recognize, unique in that one human being depends on the body of another: *all* forms of support of another human being involve our bodies in *some* sense, simply because we are bodily beings. However, some forms of bodily support are surely morally required; for example, feeding a disabled family member if he or she will otherwise die. Another example might be the case of a newborn baby who will die if not breastfed by the mother (Singer 1993: 140–1). Imagine that they live in a snowbound area and no-one else can care for the child for several months. Can the mother decline to breastfeed her baby, on the grounds that she can do what she likes with her body? Like breastfeeding, pregnancy is hardly an unusual or 'high tech' form of support. Indeed, it is much more usual than breastfeeding, given the fact that all of us received it at one time in our lives. Is pregnancy support, which all of us received, too much to ask from the mother of someone who needs it to survive?

Bodily rights

A separate point is that abortion is not, in many cases, a mere with-drawal of support: the foetus is physically attacked in order to extract it from the body of the mother. If the foetus is a human moral subject, the question arises whether we can justify this kind of bodily attack. Like other human subjects, the foetus would appear to have a right not to have its body deliberately invaded in ways which do it only lethal harm.[3]

Some bodily rights, such as our right to *move* our bodies, do not apply in many situations where we or other people will be harmed. In contrast, the right not to be physically attacked oneself is of much wider application. There is, of course, the exception of self-defence against unjust aggression. However, it seems rather strained to ascribe such aggression to the foetus in the womb, which is not only in its natural environment, but quite without aggressive intentions. The foetus should not, any more than the infant, be classed as an unjust aggressor simply because it is making the normal demands of a child of that age.

Status of the foetus

In view of these factors, it is essential, in trying to establish if abor-tion is morally justified, to look at the status of the foetus. Is the foetus a human 'person' – that is, a human individual with human moral status? If not, then abortion may be justified, not because the foetus is physically dependent on the pregnant woman but because its moral status is inferior to her own.

It was claimed in Chapter 2 that human 'persons' are simply human beings: bodily human individuals. It is hard to deny that the foetus is the *same* bodily human individual – the same human organism – as the baby who is eventually born, and the adult into which that baby grows. Like many other organisms, the human being originates very much smaller than it ends up, and goes through a lengthy period of growth and dependency. At the embryo stage, the human being looks different from how it looks as a foetus and infant; however, other organisms look different at different stages of development. It is true that the early embryo raises several puzzles, which will be discussed in the next chapter. However, it is very hard to argue that (for example) the two-month-old foetus is not the same living being as the six-month-old foetus, and as the baby who has just been born.

If the foetus is the same individual, or human being, as the newborn baby, does it also have the same moral status? As many writers on ethics have recognized, birth – a change in location *vis-à-vis* the mother's body – cannot be the threshold between those who have and those who lack human status. (Such writers will either condemn both abortion and infanticide as the killing of innocent 'persons' or human beings, or else accept both abortion and infanticide, at least in some cases, as the killing of 'non-persons'.)

Birth as a marker for human moral status does not, in fact, have much to recommend it. Nor is 'viability' – the ability of the foetus to survive outside the womb – a more plausible contender. Why should the foetus be thought to acquire a right to maternal protection just at the point when the need for such protection has become rather less acute? In any case, viability is not a fixed point, but is contingent on the current state of medical technology,[4] and on the access to such technology of babies born premature. A child born at twenty-three weeks, who is 'viable' in a hospital with very good facilities, will not be 'viable' if he or she is born a thousand miles from such facilities. Would a child in the womb at twenty-three weeks lose the moral status he or she had just acquired if the mother were to travel to a place without these facilities (Singer 1993: 140)? Why should the physical location of a child – whether in the womb or in relation to a hospital – be seen as conferring on that child a particular moral status?

In Chapters 1 and 2, we discussed the claim that 'personal' status is intrinsic to human beings. As soon as a human being exists at all, he or she has morally significant interests in the goods of human life.

A person who has been twelve months in a coma has the same interest in his or her health[5] as the person who has just fallen into a coma, or the person who has just come out. A newborn baby, like a ten-year-old child, has an interest in life and friendship, although, unlike a ten-year-old child, he or she is quite unaware of what life and friendship might be. A similar point can be made about the unborn child: he or she has interests in the 'human goods', despite his or her lack of knowledge of, and desire for, these human goods.

Mental abilities

What if we said instead that it is *current mental abilities* which give a human being interests, or interests of moral significance? One problem with this view is the fact that mental abilities come in different types and degrees.[6] We are thus faced with an unattractive set of alternatives. We could see human beings as having different moral status even as adults, depending on (for example) their intelligence. This view seems morally repugnant. Or we could draw a line at some level of achievement – but any line we draw seems quite arbitrary. Why should a six-month-old foetus have a status which the five-month-old foetus lacks? Why should a brain-damaged patient in the process of recovering some mental functions re-acquire his status at *this* point, rather than *that*, in his gradual convalescence?[7]

It could be argued that the onset of *any* current mental ability, however slight, marks the onset of human moral status. In the case of the foetus, the onset of consciousness is often seen as morally significant. However, many animals have some degree of consciousness without having (so most of us believe) the same moral status as human beings. Moreover, the conscious foetus could, perhaps, be painlessly killed – for example, by using an anaesthetic. Such a foetus would still be deprived of the goods involved in human life. But this can also be said of the foetus who dies before the point of reaching consciousness. The foetus of whatever age is a living human individual, who thus has interests in his or her future fulfilment as that kind of being.

Membership of the human kind

Like other human beings, the foetus is a member of the rational human species or 'kind'.[8] The healthy foetus shows evidence of this in its construction of a brain of a type which will eventually support rational activities. Of course, things can and do go wrong, both before and after birth. Just as an adult can be damaged to such an extent as to lack short-term rational abilities, a foetus can be damaged to such an extent as to lack the normal, unblocked potential to acquire these abilities.

What is important, however, is the fact that such a foetus is a member of the *human kind* – as can be seen from the human self-organizing powers which the foetus still retains.[9] As a member of this kind, the foetus has *interests in what fulfils* a member of this kind.[10] Even a foetus who will not, under present conditions, develop rationality is a member of this kind, with interests – including the interest in rational fulfilment – which are not shared by non-rational animals. The interests of a being depend on what constitutes that being's intrinsic fulfilment – which in turn depends on the kind of being it is. It is part of the intrinsic fulfilment of a bird – part of its health – that it be able to fly. Just as a bird, but not a human being, has an intrinsic interest[11] in acquiring and maintaining the ability to fly, so the foetus, but not the non-rational animal, has an interest in acquiring and maintaining the ability to think rationally. The ability to think rationally, in older human beings, is an aspect of health and a pre-requisite to goods such as knowledge, which in turn are aspects of human fulfilment or well-being. However, the foetus also has interests in the other 'human goods' such as friendship, in which beings of the kind to which it belongs should be able to participate.[12]

If human interests are morally significant – as most of us assume they are in the case of older human beings – then belonging to the kind of being whose members have such interests is morally significant. If it is right to respect the newborn child, as a member of the rational human kind, it is right to respect the unborn child, who is also a member of this kind. Respect for the unborn child does not require that he or she – any more than the older human being – be supported by every possible means. What it does require, if the unborn child has the same important interests as the older human being,[13] is that he or she not be deliberately attacked, negligently endangered or denied such support as it is reasonable to expect. Abortion not only involves, in many cases, a deliberate attack on the body of the foetus, but also involves the withdrawal of support of a kind which every adult has received.

Abortion and motherhood

What if a woman feels she is morally obliged – or, at least, morally entitled – to abort because she cannot meet the demands of motherhood (Hursthouse 1997: 233–4)? If the foetus is *already a child*, then it would appear that the woman already has the responsibilities of a mother. As with any mother–child relationship, these responsibilities can impose very real burdens on an individual woman. However, there is, in the case of pregnancy, simply no way of escaping these burdens without serious injustice to the child. Like the mother of the newborn baby who is alone in a snowbound area, the mother of an unborn child will need to support that child until such time as someone else can take over. Of course, unlike the situation with the snowbound mother and child, there are others who can and should help the pregnant woman: the father of the child, the woman's friends and family, and, indeed, society at large. To say that a pregnant woman has the responsibilities of a mother is not to say that she should be left to face these responsibilities alone.

It may be objected that children should not be born unwanted by their parents. Attitudes to children do, in fact, change, in many cases, as a pregnancy develops. In any event, there is no need to accept uncritically the attitude taken by the parents at the time abortion is considered. From the child's point of view, what is needed is a change of heart on the parents' part. Should parents not be prepared to want their own children – or at very least, to accept and care for their children until they can be cared for by others? Of course, we can all imagine cases in which a pregnancy would be unwelcome to anyone[14] – but do the children involved in such pregnancies have no moral claim on their parents?

A child who is unwanted by his or her parents, or by other people, does not lose his or her moral status. We might think of street children in Brazil, who are sometimes shot by vigilantes. It would be ludicrous to defend such killings on the ground that those killed are not wanted by their parents or society. Even in the worst of situations, a human being's status is not determined by the feelings of those about him or her.

Harm to the mother

With abortion as with other moral choices, it is important to think of the effect of what is chosen on the person who is choosing. If a choice involves an unjust harm, it is not only the victim who is harmed but the person who brings that harm about. Women who have undergone abortions – especially at some distance in the past – will sometimes report feelings not merely of sorrow or regret, but of guilt or remorse.[15] They feel in some way harmed by the abortion. Such harm may reveal itself in symptoms – which may or may not be recognized at first – of anger, depression, feelings of worthlessness, sexual problems and problems bonding with any subsequent child. These reactions are significant both in themselves, and as an indication of a very deep feeling, on the part of some, at least, who have abortions, that they have acted wrongly in so doing.

Apart from the harm which is, or may be, experienced by women at the moral and emotional level, there is a physical harm inherent in abortion, whatever its subsequent effects. Abortion does not merely harm the unborn child, but makes the woman's body incapable of bringing that child successfully to term. Gestation is a bodily function of considerable duration and importance; the failure to give birth to any child conceived is a failure of this bodily function. To cause this failure would appear to be a harm, at least *prima facie*. Such harm is not, of course, confined to abortion, but is found in natural miscarriage. Miscarriage, whether or not it is intended, is something which constitutes reproductive failure, not reproductive health or success.

Life-saving treatment

There are, however, cases where the woman who miscarries is already very ill. What should we say about an 'indirect' abortion, where the unborn child will die as a side-effect of life-saving treatment for the mother? For example, a miscarriage may be caused by drugs a woman needs to take for cancer. Or in the case of ectopic pregnancy, the pregnancy itself may cause a threat to the life of the woman who is pregnant. One way of treating tubal pregnancy, in particular,[16] is to remove the tube, first clamping the maternal blood vessels leading to it, even though one knows that the foetus, if it is still alive, will die as a result.

Such cases need to be examined in the light of the principle of double effect discussed in the previous chapter. Like an older human being, the foetus may sometimes be 'indirectly' (that is, non-intentionally) harmed in the course of doing something good – in this case, saving the mother's life. Of course, if the treatment can be safely delayed, or if an alternative treatment will be less harmful to the child, both the doctor and the pregnant woman should choose the option which will do less harm. Accepting side-effects is only reasonable if these side-effects are proportionate to the good expected – which they will not be if the treatment chosen does harm which can be readily avoided.

Tubal pregnancy

In the case of tubal ectopic pregnancy, where the embryo implants in the fallopian tube, there are several possible responses. If the pregnancy is diagnosed early, so that it poses no immediate threat to the woman, there is the option of 'expectant' management: that is, simply waiting for the pregnancy to miscarry naturally. This option will, in many cases, circumvent the need for surgery, which may harm the mother in addition to the child.

If the pregnancy does not miscarry, and the tube is damaged, there is the option of removing the tube, or part of the tube, with the foetus inside. Again, this option is morally acceptable: there is no objection to removing a damaged organ of the mother which is endangering her life. Such an intervention is like a hysterectomy carried out on a pregnant, but cancerous womb: the organ would need to be removed, even if the foetus had already miscarried. In the case of emergency removal of a damaged tube, or part of a tube, the foetus is likely to be very close to death, if not already dead. The threat to the mother which necessitates immediate removal of the tube is coming not from the foetus at this stage, but from the tube itself. The foetus, if it is still alive, will die at the point where its blood supply is cut off by the clamping of the maternal blood vessels leading to the tube. There is no reason why the death of the foetus, or the absence of the living foetus from the body of the woman, need be in any way intended by the doctor or the woman herself.

More problematic is the removal of the tube, or part of the tube, before the crisis intervenes, while the tube is still relatively healthy. Here it would appear that the doctor *is* intending, if not the death of the foetus, the absence of the living foetus from the body of the mother. It should, however, be noted that withdrawal of bodily support from the ectopic foetus will not constitute withdrawal of *normal* bodily support, since the support of the tube is highly abnormal and precarious for both mother and child. Whether or not such deliberate withdrawal of support is *justifiable*, it does not seem to constitute a *direct attack* on the child. The intention is, at most, to remove the foetus together with the tube, not to end its life, or invade its body in a way which can only do it harm (Watt, in preparation).

Much harder to defend are other ways of dealing with tubal pregnancy – for example, by using the drug methotrexate (MTX), which works by attacking the placenta. There are good grounds for thinking that the placenta and related tissues (the umbilical cord, the amniotic sac) are organs of the foetus.[17] If this is so, an attack on the placenta will constitute a bodily attack on the foetus itself. Such an attack may also be involved in attempts to squeeze the foetus out of the tube, if this cannot be achieved without breaking into the foetal membranes. Even if the unborn child may be deliberately removed from a place of abnormal support, he or she may not be deliberately attacked in order to achieve this. It is understandable that in such cases there may be a desire to leave the tube intact to protect the woman's future fertility. However, while this desire is in itself good, it cannot justify a direct attack on the body of the child.

The option which is morally safer, if the tube is still relatively healthy, is 'expectant' management. If the pregnancy persists and the tube is damaged, the tube, or damaged part, may be removed. If there is a possibility of giving the embryo or foetus a chance to reimplant in the uterus,[18] this would, of course, be best of all. However, in a case where the foetus cannot be saved, to remove a damaged tube is morally acceptable, even if we take it that the foetus is a child.

Rights of the pregnant woman

It may be asked why some, if not all, forms of life-saving treatment for the pregnant woman may be justified, even if no more lives will be saved by treating than by not treating. In the case of cancer, in particular, where the foetus could survive if the woman is not treated, why should a doctor intervene to ensure that the sick as opposed to the healthy patient survives? After all, we would not, presumably, be willing to tolerate a treatment of a patient in hospital which had the side-effect of causing the death of a patient nearby (say, by releasing a poisonous gas) (Foot 1978: 29). Why, then, do we feel we can accept the causation of a lethal side-effect in the case of a woman who is pregnant, and who also has cancer?

Unlike the second patient in the hospital example, the unborn child is contained within the body of the woman seeking treatment. Both the good and the bad effects of treatment take place within the outer boundaries of her body, and thus within, and/or surrounded by, her rightful sphere of influence. Of course, there are limits to this sphere of influence: the woman and her doctor may not intend to overstep, in harmful ways, the boundaries of the body of her child. However, in seeking a healing effect on the body of the woman herself, they may accept, though not intend, harm to the child which they could not accept if the person harmed were someone in the next bed.

In short, a pregnant woman does have certain rights with regard to her own body. She does not have the right to attack her own body or the body of her unborn child. Nor does she have the right to deprive her child deliberately of normal bodily support. However, she does have the right to accept at least some forms of life-saving treatment of her body, even if her unborn child will die as a side-effect of treatment she receives. A pregnant woman may choose to waive this right to save the life of her child. Such a choice is admirable[19] – indeed, heroic; it is not, however, morally required.

Chapter 5

Embryo destruction

It was claimed in the previous chapter that the foetus is a 'person' or human moral subject: the same living being, with the same moral status, as the infant and the adult. Can this also be said of the early embryo, or is the early embryo a different kind of being? If the human person is indeed the human being or organism, at every stage of life, what is the evidence that the early embryo is the same organism as the adult?

In vitro fertilization

This question often arises in the context of *in vitro* fertilization (IVF). The woman being treated, or the ovum donor, is, in most cases, given drugs to make her produce more ova than she would normally produce.[1] A number of these ova are then fertilized outside her body, thus creating human embryos. Normally, IVF involves the creation of 'spare' or 'surplus' embryos, some of which (or whom) will be frozen and/or discarded or used in experiments.

Clearly, this is not a necessary feature of IVF. It is quite possible to use only the single ovum from a woman's natural cycle, or, if more ova are retrieved, to create only as many embryos as one is intending to transfer to the body of the mother. However, the production of 'spare' embryos is certainly very common in IVF, as it is in various other forms of assisted conception. It can, indeed, be argued that a process of *production* of embryos is itself conducive to a tendency to dominate (through quality control, for example) the 'product' which results. Leaving this question aside, our concern in this chapter is with the status of the very early embryo, since this topic raises problems not raised by abortion later in development.

Status of the embryo

One of the special problems raised by the early embryo is its physical appearance. An early embryo is very small indeed; it is also quite unlike the foetus and infant in its structure and shape. It is relatively easy to empathize with a foetus, once we know what it looks like and what it can do. It is much harder to empathize with a being as alien in appearance and behaviour as the very early embryo (Grobstein 1988: 140).

These considerations are emotionally powerful, but have little rational appeal. It was claimed in the previous chapter that a human being's status does not depend on whether or not that human being is 'wanted' by the parents or by others. A corollary of this is that a human being's status does not depend on whether or not he or she is physically familiar, attractive or appealing. It would be quite unacceptable if, for example, newborn babies with disfigurements were treated as 'non-persons', on the grounds that they had less emotional appeal than other children. It is therefore arbitrary to claim that the embryo is a subhuman or subpersonal being on the grounds of its unfamiliar and/or unappealing appearance.

As we noted earlier, many organisms look different at different stages of development. A lepidopteran, for example, looks different as a caterpillar from how it looks as a butterfly. However, a caterpillar is the same living being – the same lepidopteran – as the butterfly into which it grows. In the same way, the fact that the embryo looks different from the foetus, infant and adult is not by itself enough to prove that the embryo is not a human being. Changes in structure and appearance are routine among living beings in general, and continue (albeit in lesser form) in human beings after birth. For example, children first grow and then discard their milk teeth, female children grow breasts, and so on. Such changes are produced by the organism itself, with each developmental stage actively preparing for the next stage of development. There is therefore nothing unusual in the fact that unborn children undergo changes in structure and appearance, so that (for example) they develop the placenta: an organ discarded at birth.[2]

Identical twinning

A more serious reason for denying that the embryo is the same individual as the adult is the fact that the early embryo has the potential to twin. Two human beings may result from the splitting of the embryo[3] at an early stage of development. Which of these two human beings is the embryo who existed prior to the split? If identical twinning involves a *symmetric* split, neither resulting individual will be more continuous with the original embryo than the other. The embryo cannot be the same individual as *both* the individuals who result from the split. How can we say that the embryo is the same individual as the adult into which it may develop when it may also twin, producing two individuals, with neither of whom it can be exclusively identified?[4]

The potential to twin may seem an insuperable problem; it is, however, quite compatible with the continuity of the embryo with the older human being where twinning does not take place. Where twinning does take place, the embryo either survives the process, or does not. Let us first assume that the embryo who twins splits symmetrically in half, and therefore ceases to exist in giving rise to two new individuals. What makes a human being a human being or organism is the potential it has to organize itself, or continue to organize itself, as a living human 'whole'. In the case of the embryo, this potential for human self-organization includes *developmental* potential. A conceptus would not be a genuine human embryo if it lacked the tendency to develop, in a favourable environment, into an older human being. However, if a conceptus *does* have such potential, and receives not a favourable environment but one which makes it split in half, that conceptus is still an embryo prior to splitting, and still an individual human being. Even if an embryo is in some way damaged, so that it is *predisposed* to split in half, that embryo is still a living human embryo if, in some conceivable environment, it could still develop as a living human whole. If, on the other hand, the conceptus does not have developmental potential in *any* environment, then it is not (or no longer) a living human embryo, and not a human being.

So much for a case of twinning where the embryo or conceptus is destroyed in the process. It is, however, difficult to say if identical twinning involves a symmetric split. At least some embryos may survive the process of reproducing asexually, just as adults survive the process of reproducing sexually. Indeed, an adult will also survive the process of reproducing *asexually*, if it is possible to make a clone from one of his or her cells. A clone produced from an adult would not mean that the adult was not a living human individual.

We are, of course, familiar from other areas of nature with asexual reproduction. A plant can produce a new plant if (for example) a cutting is taken; an amoeba can produce two new amoebae. Whether we see the first individual as ceasing to exist – as in the case of the amoeba – or as surviving – as in the case of the plant – the ability to generate one or more new living beings does not cast doubt on the existence of the first living being. Why, then, should the ability of the embryo to reproduce itself in certain conditions cast doubt on the embryo's existence as a living human being? Surely, what counts is not what *other* abilities or liabilities the embryo may have,[5] but whether it has the *defining* ability to develop as a living human whole.

Developmental potential

It may be objected that if an embryo is a human being – or, as some say, a 'potential human being'[6] – in view of its potential to give rise to human development, sperm and ova must also be human beings or 'potential human beings', since they share this potential (Harris 1985: 11–12; 1992: 34–7; Singer and Dawson 1988). When we look more closely at the embryo, however, we see that its potential is something quite different from the potential of the sperm and ovum from which it was created. The embryo's potential to develop is not a *passive* potential – like, for example, the potential of an apple to be picked and split in half. Rather, it is an *active* potential – a potential *to act*, while remaining the same individual (Wade 1975; Watt 1996a; Lee 1996: 24–9). Both living wholes, such as human beings, and living parts, such as sperm and ova, have active, as well as passive potential. But while the sperm and ovum have the active potential *to participate in fertilization*, whereby they cease to exist, the *embryo* has the active potential *to develop as a human individual*, given a favourable environment. That is, the embryo has the active potential to bring about developmental changes in itself, while remaining throughout the same individual human being – the same human organism. The embryo is not, in other words, a *potential* human being, any more than a newborn baby is a potential human being. Rather, in view of the embryo's potential to organize itself as a living human whole, it is an *actual* human being, who has interests in surviving and growing up as that kind of being. Like the baby, the embryo has interests in fulfilling its potential to develop, while remaining what it is. It is (for example) a potential human adult, but not a potential human being.

Fertilization

Fertilization is often said to be a process, not a moment, so that it is wrong to speak of the 'moment' of fertilization as the beginning of most, if not all, individual human lives. It is, in fact, the case that fertilization is a process, beginning when the sperm makes contact with the ovum and ending at syngamy, when the male and female chromosomes pair off inside a single cell. However, the fact that fertilization is a process does not mean there is no precise moment *during* this process[7] which marks the appearance of a new human individual. If the embryo is defined by its potential, can we not identify the moment when the relevant potential first appears to be present in an individual being? We might link this moment, in particular, to the stage at which the inside of the sperm has shed its membrane and the genetic material it contains has passed completely inside the ovum. The ovum has both an outer shell (the *zona pellucida*) and an inner cell membrane, so that the sperm first passes through the *zona* and then arrives at the inner membrane. When the two membranes open to each other, the contents of the sperm are released into the interior of the ovum (Tonti-Filippini 1992). Within a single cell there is now all the genetic material needed, from both father and mother, for development to begin. By its subsequent activity, the one-cell embryo gives evidence of developmental powers which are quite different from the powers of the entities from which it is created. As a living whole, with these defining powers, the embryo does not come into existence by degrees; rather, it immediately replaces two living parts: the ovum and the sperm.

For this reason, it is misleading to speak of the embryo as a 'fertilized ovum'. The embryo is no more a fertilized ovum than it is a fertilizing sperm. It is an entity with totally new powers, created from the interaction of two pre-existing entities. It is also worth noting that the ovum and sperm are not 'potential human beings'.[8] Rather, they are each potential, partial *causes* of a human being (Joyce 1981: 350). The same can be said of the human cells from which a clone might, in theory, be produced.

Brain life

It is sometimes said that the embryo cannot be a living human being, since it lacks a functioning brain until approximately six weeks have elapsed. If the cessation of brain activity is the criterion used to determine when a human being dies, should not the onset of brain activity be the criterion used to determine when human life begins (Brody 1976: 107–10)?

The best argument for the significance of 'brain death' as the death of a human being is that the brain is the 'integrating organ' of the (mature) human being. The brain is, in other words, necessary for the human being to organize itself as a living human whole. This argument has not gone unchallenged, some writers claiming that integrated bodily activity can persist despite a total absence of brain function.[9] Leaving this question aside, the evidence suggests that whether or not a functioning brain is required to integrate the older human being, it is not required to integrate the embryo. The embryo, in fact, gives every sign of growing and maturing as a living human whole – not least, by developing the brain which will integrate, or help to integrate, bodily activities later in gestation. Brain development is, in short, just another way in which a transformation of structure and function can take place in the life of one and the same living individual.

Natural embryo wastage

It is sometimes claimed that embryos cannot have human status, in view of the fact that many embryos fail to implant in the natural course of events. Exactly what proportion fail to implant is a matter of dispute; moreover, some conceptuses which fail to implant will not be human embryos, as they do not have a human genetic constitution.[10] In the case of those who *are* human embryos, the likelihood of death by natural causes does not seem relevant to the permissibility of the *deliberate killing* of those naturally at risk. Nature, unlike human beings, is not a moral agent. It should be remembered that the rate of *infant* mortality has been very high for most of human history, and is very high today in some developing countries. Notwithstanding this, children in such countries have the same moral status as children in developed countries, who have a better chance of survival. A child who may die early still needs to be cared for, and should on no account be deliberately killed on the grounds that his or her life is already at risk.

Implications of the embryo's status

There are, then, arguments in favour of the embryo's continuity, both in being and in status, with the older human individual. If the embryo has, or may well have, the same moral status as the older human being, what are the moral implications? If it is wrong to kill an innocent human being, and the embryo is, or may well be, an innocent human being, then there is much to object to in the practice of *in vitro* fertilization. It is a matter of very great concern that embryos are mass-produced *in vitro* and, in many cases, discarded or used in research. Parents should be prepared, in advance of conception, to accept their children unconditionally; they should not conceive children with the aim of 'selecting out' those they do not want. Freezing is not a satisfactory solution, since freezing, while it does save some embryos, destroys many others. Moreover, even those embryos who survive the freezing process may never have a chance to go to term, either because their parents do not want them or because, in some countries, the law requires them to be thawed and discarded after a certain period of time.

Human cloning

Of course, some embryos are specifically created for research, and not for implantation. Hitherto, embryos have mostly been created for this purpose by means of IVF. However, there is now considerable interest in creating embryos for research by means of cloning. An ovum deprived of its nucleus will be given the nucleus of some other cell, in the hope that the entity resulting will develop as a new human embryo. Such an embryo will be the clone or twin of the person who provided the cell from which the nucleus was taken. The embryo created by 'tissue' or 'therapeutic' cloning, as it is described,[11] can then be used in research and, eventually, as a source of spare parts. In the future, children or adults could be provided with a clone who would serve them as a living bank of transplant material (Harris 1992: 104–7).[12] Clearly, if the embryo is a human moral subject, with rights and interests in its human future, such a procedure will be morally quite indefensible.

Abortifacient 'contraceptives'

Cloning and IVF are not, however, the only areas in which the status of the very early embryo has practical importance. One disturbing implication of the view that the embryo is a human moral subject is that many so-called contraceptives will have to be described as potentially homicidal. These include IUDs and the 'morning after' pill, which are advertised – somewhat misleadingly – as contraceptives, not abortifacients. They also include, unknown to many women, oral contraceptives in standard doses, which work at least sometimes by preventing any embryo conceived after 'breakthrough' ovulation from implanting in the womb.[13] Of course, women who are unaware, through no fault of their own, of the fact that this is so are in no way morally responsible for any death they cause by taking oral contraceptives. However, women who are aware of this fact, and who suspect that the embryo is, or may be, a young human being will undoubtedly have grounds for thinking they should choose some other form of family planning.

Non-abortifacient forms of family planning include barrier methods such as the condom, and methods of natural family planning[14] such as the Billings and symptothermal methods, and use of devices such as the Persona to determine when the woman is fertile. It has to be said here that non-hormonal methods are not all morally equivalent. Spermicides, for example, in addition to other problems will double the risk of miscarriage of a pregnancy which follows their use (Wilks 1997: 126).[15] However, objections to non-hormonal methods, where they do exist, will largely concern not the risk of miscarriage but other issues beyond the scope of this book.[16]

Chapter 6

Cooperation

It will by now be clear from the cases we have discussed – if it were not already clear from our experience – that people disagree profoundly with regard to life and death questions in healthcare. Such disagreement does not, however, indicate – as some might be tempted to believe – that questions such as these have no true answers. After all, people also disagree profoundly with regard to questions we see as clearly factual: for example, with regard to past events.

However, it must be admitted that disagreement on moral issues tends to be more serious in its implications than many other forms of disagreement. It is, for example, important in healthcare that patients are treated with the respect they deserve; lack of consensus as to what counts as such respect is clearly a matter for concern.

Moral disagreement poses special problems for those who find themselves outside the mainstream position in their profession. Healthcare workers, in particular, may find themselves under pressure to conform to the requirements of those who do not recognize what these individuals see as moral problems. Pressure may range from, in extreme cases, threats of dismissal or non-promotion to more subtle but nonetheless unpleasant expressions of disapproval, ridicule or dislike.

However, even those whose colleagues are sympathetic to their general position of conscientious objection may be uncertain to what lengths this position should be taken in their work. If a doctor or nurse believes (for example) that abortion is morally wrong – or even that *some* abortions are morally wrong – what should the doctor or nurse do if asked to cooperate in what he or she sees as an immoral procedure? Cooperation may range from taking part in the abortion (for example, handing instruments to the doctor who performs it), to giving premedication or post-abortion care or filling in the necessary forms.

Formal and material cooperation

The first distinction we need to make in the area of cooperation is between *formal* and *material* cooperation. In Chapter 3 we looked at the distinction between what we aim at and what we merely foresee: a distinction which can be morally significant. It was noted that our choices generally have some bad effects, and that it is sometimes permissible to foresee and accept an effect which we do not and may not intend. *Material* cooperation in the wrongful actions of others, where these actions are foreseen, but not intended, by the person who cooperates, should be seen as one area in which accepting side-effects is sometimes permissible.[1]

Formal cooperation in the wrongful actions of others occurs where the person cooperating intends to help the principal agent in doing precisely what is wrong. In the case of abortion, a person who hands instruments to the doctor performing the abortion can, in practice, be assumed to share the doctor's intention that the abortion take place.[2] If it is wrong to have or perform an abortion oneself, it is also wrong to intend (as opposed to foresee) that someone else will have or perform an abortion. That other person will, after all, be doing exactly the same thing which it would be wrong to do oneself.

Justifying material cooperation

Formal cooperation in wrongful procedures is, then, morally excluded. How should we go about judging cases of *material* cooperation, where we do not intend, but merely foresee, that what we do will somehow contribute to some wrongful procedure? Material cooperation can range from very close cooperation (giving premedication)[3] to very remote cooperation (keeping the hospital generator going). Some forms of cooperation will be so remote as to be unproblematic; others will be close enough to raise objections which are decisive in that case. Close material cooperation is likely to be unjust to those whom one is, in effect, helping to harm (in the case of abortion, the unborn child, the mother and others who are choosing the abortion). Such cooperation is likely to give a strong, even if unwarranted, impression that one agrees with, or does not strongly *disagree* with, the injustice being done. It is difficult to convince our colleagues that we have a serious objection to abortion if we are prepared to wheel patients into the room where abortions are performed. On the other hand, some forms of cooperation – for example, caring for patients *after* abortion – have some connection with the abortion but are less likely to suggest that our objection to it is weak or insincere.

Occasionally, there will be a very strong reason to refuse to cooperate even remotely in some unjust procedure, because by refusing it is possible to stop that procedure taking place. However, it will normally be the case that the wrongful procedure will be carried out whether or not we ourselves are in any way involved. If this is so, we need to compare, once again, the reasons for cooperating and the reasons for not cooperating. These reasons include the harm done, to ourselves and others, by either course of action. Refusal to cooperate may involve ourselves and our families in unpleasant consequences by (for example) costing us our jobs. On the other hand, cooperating – even remotely – in an unjust procedure may harm us, in that it may dull our sensitivities towards the wrong involved in that procedure. It may, for example, make us more inclined to cooperate more closely – perhaps even formally – in the future. It may also harm other people, in that it may give them the impression that the wrong concerned is not, after all, so very wrong in our eyes.

The greater the risk of corrupting ourselves, or of giving the impression to others that we do not object, or do not object very strongly, to some wrongful procedure, the more serious needs to be the reason for doing what facilitates this procedure. One possible, though admittedly not infallible, test, where the procedure takes a human life unjustly, is to ask what we would do if it were our own lives at stake, or the lives of those we love. Passing an instrument to someone I know is going to use it to kill me or someone in my family is something I might be prepared to do at gunpoint, but not to avoid losing my job. If so, should I be prepared to pass an instrument which will be used to kill an unborn child,[4] simply to avoid losing my job? In fact, the question should not arise: conscientious refusal to participate this closely in abortion operations is, in many countries, protected by law. However, there is, of course, no guarantee that the legal rights of health professionals will always correspond to their moral rights and duties to refuse participation.

Moral integrity revisited

The demands of morality on healthcare workers can seem intolerably hard, especially for those who find themselves in a minority position in their profession. In regard to these demands, there are certain points we need to bear in mind. First, there is the fact that good actions, like bad actions, are 'habit-forming': the more we do difficult things, the less difficult we are likely to find them. Conversely, of course, the less we do what is morally required of us in certain situations, the less likely we are to do so in similar situations in the future.

Second, this effect of actions on our character is (as we saw in Chapter 3) quite central to morality. Good and bad actions have an impact on the kind of people we become. Actions involving unjust harm, or unduly close cooperation in such harm, not only harm the most obvious victim, but those who do the harm or help the harm-doer. In contrast, refusing to do such harm, or to cooperate too closely in it, benefits us, and may also benefit those with whom we have to work. In any case, our first responsibility is to act with integrity ourselves. We are not responsible for what we are unable to prevent; we are, however, responsible for the kind of people we make ourselves by what we choose to do.

Finally, it should be remembered that conscientious objection may be easier psychologically if we can give good reasons to our colleagues for taking the position we do. While it is certainly possible to refuse cooperation without going into our reasons in detail, it is normally easier if we can provide a rational account of our refusal. Such an account will normally include an account of what is wrong with the procedure in which we are refusing to participate. It is such an account, with regard to procedures such as euthanasia, abortion and embryo destruction, which I have tried to give, in summary form, in the course of this book.

Notes

Introduction

1 For an introduction to arguments for and against the objectivity of ethics, see Benn 1998: 1–58.
2 In this book, the terms 'moral' and 'ethical' will be used interchangeably.

Chapter 1

1 Deaths can also be physically caused by an omission. For example, I can stay where I am on the footpath in rush-hour, omitting to move, with the result that people bump into me and fall onto the road. This seems harder to defend than failing to pull people *off* the road, but easier to defend than knocking them onto the road as I walk past.

   Some writers have argued that the causing/allowing distinction, but not the act/omission distinction, is morally significant (Foot 1985: 24; Denyer 1997: 43). The two distinctions can perhaps be brought together, if degrees of causal involvement are seen as having moral relevance. If I fail to move in the rush-hour case, my causal involvement with those who fall onto the road is greater than if I failed to pull them off the road when they were already on it. It is, however, less than if I made some external movement – such as walking past – which knocked them off the kerb.

2 Of course, deliberate omissions are also 'acting', in the sense that they are chosen behaviour.

3 A similar case is discussed in Rachels 1979: 493–4.

4 Natural events such as earthquakes are evaluated in relation to their *outputs* (that is, their results). In contrast, human actions are evaluated *morally* in relation to their *inputs*: in relation to the intentions and other states of mind which they express. Intentions are what make a human action subject to moral assessment in the first place; particular intentions have a further influence on how that action is assessed (Garcia 1992: 239–41).

5 Alternatively, the person threatened might wrongly intend the child's death as a means of escaping death himself. In such cases of duress, culpability will, however, be reduced.

6 The term 'worth living' is normally used to mean 'worth living for the individual whose life it is'. This is not to say that a life cannot also be 'worth living' for (as well as to) other people, in the sense that it is, in some objective sense, beneficial or potentially beneficial to these other people.

7 Michael Tooley, who considers this kind of example in a series of publications (Tooley 1972, 1974, 1983), has progressively modified his position on the connection between interests and desires. He now holds that a being can have non-momentary interests if it can have desires at different times. These desires must, he stipulates, belong not merely to the same organism but to the same 'subject of consciousness' (1983: 120). For a critique of Tooley's present and past positions, see Lee 1996: 7–45. See also Chapter 2 of this book, for a brief defence of the view that the human organism is itself the subject of interests and (when healthy and mature) of desires.

8 There is, however, a connection, on the 'objective' view of interests, between interests and what *should* be desired.

9 Grisez *et al.* 1987 maintain that a human good may never be deliberately attacked. However, it can be argued that the relationship between the human goods and moral norms is more complex than this, so that (for example) life – or, at least, health – may be attacked in the case of an unjust aggressor.

10 The term 'killing' will often be used in this book to refer to bringing about death by omission as well as by 'positive act'. On the moral difference, if any, between 'killing' by positive act and 'letting die' by omission, see pp. 6–7, 40–2.

11 The term 'utilitarianism' is often used to refer to consequentialism where the good to be promoted is happiness, pleasure or preference satisfaction.

12 I am referring here to consequentialism of the 'goodness maximizing' kind. Consequentialism is also sometimes said to include the position of 'satisficers', who believe one should do what will bring about 'enough' good, even if more good than this could be achieved.

13 Pleasures or preferences will often be counted up 'neutrally' by consequentialists, without any moral examination. However, this seems morally objectionable. Why should (for example) the pleasures or preferences of sadists in regard to the suffering of others count for anything at all? On this point, see Smart 1973: 25–6; Benn 1998: 65–7.

14 For some consequentialist defences of infanticide, see Singer 1993: 181–91; 1994: 210–17; Glover 1977: 150–69.

15 'Total' consequentialists believe that we should maximize good both by affecting existing lives and by bringing new lives into existence. Lives are containers of (for example) pleasure; increasing the number of such containers will sometimes be what we need to do to maximize pleasure in the world. In contrast, 'prior existence' consequentialists believe that we should maximize pleasure (or something else good) only by affecting those lives which already exist, or will exist independently of our actions (Singer 1993: 103–5).

16 To arrive at the conclusion that good will be maximized by 'replacing' the Down's child with a child who does not have Down's, the consequentialist will need to find some reason why the parent or parents cannot simply have another child. 'Total' consequentialists (see note 15) will sometimes suggest that it is enough if the child is replaced by one whose life will contain (for example) more pleasure (Singer 1993: 186, 188–91). However, it is hard to see how the consequentialist wrong done by ending a happy life can be cancelled out by doing what one should be doing anyway, according to total consequentialism: increasing the number of happy lives (Hursthouse 1987: 149–53, 157–8). It is, in any case, bizarre to see a human life as a replaceable container of pleasure, as if it is the pleasure which is morally important, while the human being is not.

17 I am thinking here of act consequentialism, where the aim is to maximize in every situation.

18 Of course, it is always open to the consequentialist to argue that more good will come about if people adopt a non-consequentialist approach to making choices (see e.g. Railton 1988). Such a view places the consequentialist in the paradoxical position of defending a moral theory which cannot be used as a guide to making moral decisions. Moreover, to the extent to which we accept, on the theoretical level, the view that *consequentialism* is the correct moral theory, we undermine in ourselves the whole-hearted adoption of a non-consequentialist approach in our own moral lives (Williams 1985: 109–10).

19 For a discussion of value comparison, see Chang 1997.

20 There is, of course, a sense in which any moral system intended to guide a person's actions is 'agent relative', in that it makes moral demands on the person who is acting. Consequentialism, for example, directs the moral agent to maximize good himself and not (where this conflicts) to maximize the maximizings of others (Denyer 1997: 49–50). However, the demands on the agent, in the case of consequentialism, are simply those

of maximizing good. In contrast, in the case of non-consequentialist moral theories, it matters *how* the agent is involved in promoting good outcomes.

21 The moral agent may be so corrupt that his character cannot be further damaged by a certain kind of wrongful action. Even in this case, however, the agent can be said to be harmed by further actions of the relevant kind. Not only has his character not been retrieved from its present damaged condition, but his guilt (as opposed to his *sense* of guilt) has been further increased. There may also be other kinds of harm: e.g. to relationships with others, if we assume that good relationships with others are in a person's interests.

22 I am not suggesting that a person who refrains from unjust actions (for example) must or should be thinking about his own character when he does so. His focus may rather be on the harm such actions do to others ('How can I do that to this person?').

23 It is often suggested that there could be a 'threshold' system, whereby a person would be obliged or permitted to torture or kill whenever the harm of refusing rose above a certain point (Williams 1973: 90–1, 117–18). This position is not normally described as 'consequentialist', though it was so described by Elizabeth Anscombe in her influential paper 'Modern moral philosophy' (Anscombe 1958). While this position shows some appreciation of the role of agent-relativity, it can be argued that it does not give this factor the importance it deserves. That I behave justly (for example) is my business, even in extreme situations, in a way in which other people's just or unjust behaviour is not. Morality is about input, not, primarily, about output (see p. 16).

24 The non-consequentialist may see the term 'harmful' as already having *prima facie* practical significance, in the sense that there is some objective reason to prevent what it describes. Harmful just *means*, in this context, what it is reasonable to prevent, other things being equal.

25 See note 10.

Chapter 2

1 A strong critique has been mounted by some writers both of protocols for diagnosing brain death and of the equation of brain death with death of the organism as a whole. See e.g. Shewmon 1997, 1998; McCullagh 1993; Byrne and Nilges 1993.

2 It may be objected that a person is not a purely material being either. However, those who believe in the existence of a soul which can survive a person's death need not believe that the soul itself is the human being or person. For an account of the soul as the body's 'life principle', which nonetheless survives the body's death, see e.g. Braine 1993.

3 Any mental abilities arising after surgery would at least *appear* to be acquired by the human being or organism who undergoes the surgery. If

this is so, should we say that there are now *two* individuals coexisting with these abilities – the human being who undergoes the surgery and the 'person' the surgery creates? This seems highly implausible.

4 In fact, most people do behave, at least sometimes, as if these things were in themselves worthwhile. Most people have some experience of curiosity, the desire to make and maintain friendships and concern for their own and others' lives (say, when negotiating traffic). People will often attribute an importance to the 'human goods' – at least in reflective moments – which they do not attribute to other common objects of desire such as pleasure, wealth and power.

5 A life could be regarded as good for other people (see Chapter 1, note 6), though not for the human being him or herself.

6 Of course, the human being who has been harmed by death does not, unlike the human being harmed in other ways, go on existing as a living human being in a state of deprivation. However, the human being who dies has still been deprived of a good – continued life – even though he or she does not presently exist as a harmed human being.

7 It should, however, be noted that heart transplants will be inappropriate for patients in *any* condition, if death in the donor is not correctly diagnosed (see note 1).

8 It can be argued that there is a value attached not merely to health – that is, to the *presence* of normal bodily functions – but to the *use* of these functions in promoting human well-being. It is better, for example, other things being equal, that people feed themselves normally, rather than by gastrostomy or nasogastric tube. The bypassing of normal functions involved in both medicine and nursing is thus in some way unfortunate, however necessary it may be.

9 This statement needs to be qualified, in view of the fact that medicine and nursing in general share the 'higher' goal of keeping the patient comfortable. This goal is normally present in basic nursing care, except where the patient is unconscious.

10 One possibility would be to see the insertion of the tube as medical treatment – albeit of a very simple kind – and subsequent feeding by means of the tube as basic nursing care.

11 Carers may be nurses in a hospital or relatives at home, where many PVS patients are cared for.

Chapter 3

1 Some have defended not merely *non-voluntary* euthanasia but *involuntary* euthanasia of a competent person who has not consented to it, in a case where death is believed to be overwhelmingly in that person's interest (Singer 1993: 200–1).

2 For an account of the 'practical' slide from voluntary to non-voluntary and involuntary euthanasia in the Netherlands, see Keown 1995: 261–96; Jochemsen and Keown 1999: 16–21.

3 Counselling, for example, may be needed no less urgently than help with pain control. It is significant that Mrs Boyes lost the will to live when she became depressed after the death of a close relative (Alison Davis, personal communication).

4 See e.g. Gormally 1994: 135–6.

5 The following sections include material previously published (Watt 1996b; 1998).

6 Conversely, of course, parents may find themselves obliged to accept burdensome treatments for themselves which would not be morally required were it not for their responsibility to the children in their care. There will, however, be limits to what such parents are obliged to undergo for the sake of their children's welfare.

7 Whether such emotional reactions are sufficient to justify refusal of amputation will depend on the benefits this treatment is expected to bring. A degree of repugnance which is sufficient to justify refusal of amputation by an elderly patient with a limited life-expectancy may not be sufficient to justify refusal by a younger and/or healthier patient.

8 The decision to withdraw existing treatment from a patient is often seen as morally identical to a decision to withhold the treatment in the first place. It can, however, be argued that to be in receipt of a treatment gives one a *prima facie* claim on that treatment (Sulmasy and Sugarman 1994). We should not assume that it is *always* permissible, although it is certainly *sometimes* permissible, to withdraw a treatment on the grounds that someone else would derive from it somewhat more benefit.

9 There is, however, a sense in which curing the second illness, although misconceived, is not *altogether* futile, in that someone with two fatal illnesses is even less healthy than someone with one.

10 Patients will sometimes refuse medical treatments not because these treatments are seen as too burdensome, in any standard sense, but because they are seen as raising moral or religious objections. For example, Jehovah's Witnesses may refuse blood transfusions without which they will or may die. These refusals, too, should be respected by doctors and nurses, as refusals of a competent patient which are not suicidally motivated.

11 The life of an organism is its existence with the defining tendency to function as a whole. Health is existence with the tendency to function well, both at the macro and the micro level.

12 For discussion of the principle, see Finnis 1991: 32–64; Gormally 1994: 48–50; Garcia 1997: 161–81. See also Boyle 1991, and other papers in this issue; Foot 1978, 1985.

13 Doctors may, however, have a duty to do this for a limited period in a time of crisis (for example, in the wake of some natural disaster).

14 In most cases, the use of palliative drugs is more likely to extend than to shorten a patient's life, as the patient is more rested (Twycross 1994: 562).

15 That the intention is not to shorten life can be shown by the fact that, without inconsistency, the doctor giving the drugs could take steps to make death less likely. In contrast, a doctor who performs euthanasia could not take such steps without inconsistency, since death is the point of what she does.

16 On the subject of lethal bodily invasions without the intention to kill, see Watt, in preparation.

17 It is sometimes justified to perform a bodily invasion which only harms the person whose body is invaded, if the harm done is minor and temporary – as when, for example, blood or bone marrow is taken from a donor.

18 See Chapter 1, note 21.

19 For a discussion of 'virtue ethics', see e.g. MacIntyre 1981; Garcia 1990; Crisp and Slote 1997.

20 As Garcia points out (1997: 174), the importance of intention, as a form of 'morally significant favouring', is reflected in what we ourselves want from others. We do not simply want other people to *affect* us in good ways, but to have good attitudes towards us.

Chapter 4

1 This is argued, for example, in Thomson 1971. Thomson's article has been much discussed in the literature. See, in particular, Finnis 1973; Hursthouse 1987: 81–208; Beckwith 1992.

2 Not all feminists defend abortion; see e.g. Kennedy 1997.

3 See pp. 41–2.

4 'Viability' will, indeed, be pushed back to conception, if it ever becomes possible to gestate a child for nine months in an artificial uterus.

5 It is, of course, important, for practical purposes, to determine which of someone's interests can be *promoted* in a given situation. As we saw in Chapter 2, there are some interventions which would not be appropriate for a PVS patient, precisely because many aspects of his or her well-being cannot now be achieved.

6 Whether or not an ability is 'current' is also a matter of degree. A person who has been temporarily knocked out has 'more current' mental abilities than a person who has suffered brain-damage which will take weeks or months to heal. However, it is difficult to see why it should follow that the interests of the first person are more important morally than those of the second. A difference in the degree of 'currentness' of potential cannot bear the moral weight which is sometimes put on it (Lee 1996: 26).

7 If moral status is linked to current mental abilities, we are faced with the problem that such abilities may come and go several times in the course of someone's life. Indeed, we can imagine situations in which they would come and go several times in the course of one hour – for example, in the

course of a complex operation to restore mental function. It seems odd to suggest that the patient in this case is dependent on the surgeon not merely to *recognize* his or her status as a person, but to *confer* this status by carrying out certain interventions.

8 Our concern here is with *human* persons; however, there could, in principle, be non-human persons such as extraterrestrials with a similar moral status to our own. Such persons would be members of a rational kind of being, even if not currently able to reason themselves (due to illness, immaturity, etc.).

9 See pp. 59, 62–3.

10 The view of human beings as members of a single 'kind', for whom certain states are good and bad (healthy and unhealthy), is integral to healthcare, in particular.

11 One might want to argue that human beings would have an interest in being able to fly under certain conditions – for example, if confronted by some danger. However, this interest, if such it can be called, is purely instrumental, rather than intrinsic; it is not part of our healthy functioning as human beings that we have the capacity to fly. I am assuming here that we would retain our identity after acquiring this capacity. To speak of an interest in survival, served by an instrumental interest in flying, presupposes that we would, in fact, survive.

12 It is true that foetuses – and, indeed, infants – cannot be wronged in certain ways in which adults can be wronged by being killed. Adults will normally have worthwhile projects, such as ongoing friendships, which can be thwarted if their lives are curtailed. However, an adult who is suicidally depressed may have no such worthwhile projects. Such an adult can nonetheless, like the foetus and the infant, be unjustly and deliberately deprived of a life which is objectively worthwhile. It should be noted that the life of the foetus and infant may be of greater expected duration than that of (for example) a non-depressed septuagenarian, who has more in her life to interrupt.

13 Interests are, however, specified to some degree as a person grows up. For example, the general interest in having successful relationships with others will come to include the more specific interest in the success of relationships already formed.

14 Pregnancy following rape is, of course, one notorious example. Even in this case, however, the unborn child can be seen as a young human being whose life must be respected. To kill the innocent is not an acceptable response to the crimes of the guilty; nor is it the best way of dealing with the trauma of the victim of rape (Makhorn and Dolan 1981; Reardon 1987: 188–219). There is evidence that women are more likely to be emotionally disturbed by abortion the greater their emotional distress at the time of presentation for the abortion. See Zolese and Blacker 1992, and the references cited in Reardon 1996: 163.

15 See e.g. Reardon 1987; Zolese and Blacker 1992; Doherty 1995; Spencer 1997.

16 Not all ectopic ('out of place') pregnancies are tubal. Ectopic pregnancies come in various forms (abdominal, ovarian, etc.). Some ectopic pregnancies can proceed to viability, following which a live baby can be surgically delivered.

17 These tissues are developed by the embryo, are normally genetically those of the embryo 'proper', and serve the needs of the embryo and foetus for food, oxygen and shelter. In the case of chimeras (see Chapter 5, note 5) these tissues can be genetically different from those of the embryo 'proper' – but the embryo 'proper' can also be composed of different genetic contributions. And while it is true that these tissues can be shared by twins, the same can be said of other organs in the case of Siamese twins.

18 Birth following transfer of an ectopic embryo has been reported several times in the medical literature (Stabile 1996: 152–3).

19 Here I am assuming that the child will die if the treatment is accepted by the pregnant woman, and will live if the treatment is refused. I am also assuming that the choice to refuse it, which goes beyond the call of duty, does not conflict with any duties of the woman (e.g. to the rest of her family).

Chapter 5

1 These drugs carry medical risks for the woman; see e.g. Wilks 1997: 139–51.

2 See Chapter 4, note 17.

3 All embryos divide many times in the course of their development. However, such division normally produces not two (or more) functionally independent beings, but rather, cells which cooperate as parts of one and the same individual. Twinning is thus the exception that proves the rule with regard to cellular cooperation.

4 See Ford 1988: 120–2. For a critique of this and other arguments of Ford, see Fisher 1991.

5 Another ability or 'passive potential' of embryos is the potential to be absorbed by other embryos, so as to form chimeras (individuals with a composite genetic makeup). Again, this potential is compatible with the *active* potential to survive and develop as an embryo in a different environment.

6 Or a 'potential human person'.

7 In the same way, dying can be seen as a process, and death as an event, occurring when the organism loses, completely and beyond recovery, the active potential to organize itself as a whole.

8 Some writers have drawn attention to the phenomenon of parthenogenesis – by which is meant an embryo arising from the mere stimulation of

an ovum (Harris 1992: 35–6). If parthenogenesis is possible in humans, does not an ovum on its own already have developmental potential? In fact, there is some doubt whether the parthenogenetic conceptus is an embryo, in view of the abnormal features it displays. In any case, even if an ovum could be stimulated so as to give rise to genuine human development, the ovum would not be the same individual, with the same developmental powers, as the embryo it is used to create. Not until the structure of the ovum was radically changed by external forces would development take place.

9 See Chapter 2, note 1.

10 For example, the complete hydatiform mole formed from one or more sperm and an ovum which loses the female nucleus will give rise to placental tissue only, and is not a human embryo (Suarez 1990).

11 If the clone is intended to be transferred to the body of a woman and allowed to develop, this is known as 'reproductive' cloning.

12 Transplant material can, of course, be taken from the foetus as well as from the embryo, whether after cloning or IVF or after natural conception. Harris has argued that it would be permissible for a woman to become pregnant deliberately so as to abort the foetus and so provide tissue for use in transplantation. It would, he suggests, be permissible to do this either on altruistic grounds or with a commercial motivation (Harris 1992: 110, 129–31). On the use of foetal tissue in transplantation, see McCullagh 1987, 1993.

13 The mini-pill, in particular, fails to prevent ovulation in 40 per cent of women (Wilks 1997: 9).

14 Natural family planning (NFP) involves the observation of physical signs of the fertile period in the woman's menstrual cycle. Intercourse may then be chosen or avoided, depending on whether a pregnancy is desired. See e.g. Ryder 1993, and subsequent correspondence.

15 Barrier methods also carry a 140 per cent greater risk of the woman developing pre-eclampsia in pregnancy, due to the fact that the female immune system does not have a chance to develop gradual tolerance to male antigens on sperm and seminal fluid (Wilks 1997: 135–7).

16 For example, it can be argued that sex using contraception, unlike sex at times which are naturally infertile, lacks the kind of acceptance of fertility which promotes acceptance of children. For a range of arguments against contraceptive family planning, see Smith 1993.

Chapter 6

1 For a discussion of problems of cooperation, see Grisez 1997: 849–97. See also Fitzpatrick 1988: 128–34, 147–51, 261–4, 269–70.

2 While this could, in theory, constitute very close material cooperation, in normal circumstances it is almost certain to constitute formal cooperation, as a matter of psychological probability. See Garcia 1997: 163–6.
3 Giving premedication will, of course, constitute formal cooperation if the nurse who gives it intends to help the operation take place. However, if she simply 'does what she is told', without concerning herself with what follows, her action will constitute (unjustified) material cooperation.
4 See note 2.

Bibliography

Andrews, K., Murphy, L. and Manday, R. (1996) 'Misdiagnosis of the vegetative state: retrospective study in a rehabilitation unit', *British Medical Journal*, 313: 13–16.

Anscombe, G. E. M. (1958) 'Modern moral philosophy', *Philosophy*, 33: 1–19; reprinted in R. Crisp and M. Slote (eds) (1997) *Virtue Ethics*, New York: Oxford University Press.

Beckwith, F. J. (1992) 'Personal bodily rights, abortion and unplugging the violinist', *International Philosophical Quarterly*, 32: 105–18.

Benn, P. (1998) *Ethics*, London: UCL Press.

Borthwick, C. (1996) 'The permanent vegetative state: ethical crux, medical fiction?', *Issues in Law and Medicine*, 12: 167–85.

Boyle, J. (1991) 'Who is entitled to double effect?', *Journal of Medicine and Philosophy*, 16, 5: 475–94.

Braine, D. (1993) *The Human Person: Animal and Spirit*, London: Duckworth.

Brody, B. (1976) *Abortion and the Sanctity of Human Life: A Philosophical View*, Cambridge MA: MIT Press.

Byrne, P. and Nilges, R. (1993) 'The brain stem in brain death: a critical review', *Issues in Law and Medicine*, 9, 1: 3–21.

Chang, R. (ed.) (1997) *Incommensurability, Incomparability and Practical Reason*, Cambridge MA: MIT Press.

Crisp, R. and Slote, M. (eds) (1997) *Virtue Ethics*, New York: Oxford University Press.

Denyer, N. (1997) 'Is anything absolutely wrong?', in D. Oderberg and J. Laing (eds) *Human Lives: Critical Essays on Consequentialist Bioethics*, Basingstoke and London: Macmillan.

Doherty, P. (ed.) (1995) *Post-Abortion Syndrome*, Dublin: Four Courts Press.

Finnis, J. (1973) 'The rights and wrongs of abortion', *Philosophy and Public Affairs*, 2, 2; reprinted in M. Cohen, T. Nagel and T. Scanlon (eds) (1974) *The Rights and Wrongs of Abortion*, Princeton: Princeton University Press.

—— (1991) 'Intentions and side-effects', in R. Frey and C. Morris (eds) *Liability and Responsibility: Essays in Law and Morals*, Cambridge: Cambridge University Press.

—— (1995) 'A philosophical case against euthanasia', in J. Keown (ed.) *Euthanasia Examined: Ethical, Clinical and Legal Perspectives*, Cambridge: Cambridge University Press.

Finnis, J., Boyle, J. and Grisez, G. (1987) *Nuclear Deterrence, Morality and Realism*, Oxford: Oxford University Press.

Fisher, A. (1991) 'Individuogenesis and a recent book by Fr Norman Ford', *Anthropotes*, 7, 2: 199–235.

Fitzpatrick, F. J. (1988) *Ethics in Nursing Practice*, London: Linacre Centre.

Foot, P. (1978) 'The problem of abortion and the doctrine of double effect', in P. Foot, *Virtues and Vices*, Oxford: Blackwell.

—— (1985) 'Morality, action and outcome', in T. Honderich (ed.) *Morality and Objectivity*, London: Routledge & Kegan Paul.

Ford, N. (1988) *When Did I Begin?*, Cambridge: Cambridge University Press.

Garcia, J. L. A. (1990) 'The primacy of the virtuous', *Philosophia*, 20: 69–91.

—— (1992) 'The right and the good', *Philosophia*, 21: 235–56.

—— (1993) 'The new critique of anti-consequentialist moral theory', *Philosophical Studies*, 71: 1–32.

—— (1997) 'Intentions in medical ethics', in D. Oderberg and J. Laing (eds) *Human Lives: Critical Essays on Consequentialist Bioethics*, Basingstoke and London: Macmillan.

Glover, J. (1977) *Causing Death and Saving Lives*, Harmondsworth: Penguin.

Gormally, L. (ed.) (1994) *Euthanasia, Clinical Practice and the Law*, London: Linacre Centre.

Grisez, G. (1997) *Difficult Moral Questions*, Quincy IL: Franciscan Press.

Grisez, G., Boyle, J. and Finnis, J. (1987) 'Practical principles, moral truth, and ultimate ends', *American Journal of Jurisprudence*, 32: 99–151.

Grobstein, G. (1988) *Science and the Unborn*, New York: Basic Books.

Harris, J. (1985) *The Value of Life*, London: Routledge & Kegan Paul.

—— (1992) *Wonderwoman and Superman: The Ethics of Human Biotechnology*, Oxford: Oxford University Press.

—— (1995) 'Euthanasia and the value of life', in J. Keown (ed.) *Euthanasia Examined: Ethical, Clinical and Legal Perspectives*, Cambridge: Cambridge University Press.

Hursthouse, R. (1987) *Beginning Lives*, Oxford: Blackwell.

—— (1997) 'Virtue theory and abortion', in R. Crisp and M. Slote (eds) *Virtue Ethics*, New York: Oxford University Press.

Jochemsen, H. and Keown, J. (1999) 'Voluntary euthanasia under control? Further empirical evidence from the Netherlands', *Journal of Medical Ethics*, 25: 16–21.

Joyce, R. (1981) 'When does a person begin?', in T. W. Hilgers, D. J. Horan and D. Mall (eds) *New Perspectives on Human Abortion*, Frederick MD: University Publications of America.

Kennedy, A. (ed.) (1997) *Swimming against the Tide: Feminist Dissent on the Issue of Abortion*, Dublin: Open Air.

Keown, J. (1995) 'Euthanasia in the Netherlands: Sliding Down the Slippery Slope?', in J. Keown (ed.) *Euthanasia Examined: Ethical, Clinical and Legal Perspectives*, Cambridge: Cambridge University Press.

Lee, P. (1996) *Abortion and Unborn Human Life*, Washington: Catholic University of America Press.

Lightfoot, L. and Rogers, L. (1996) ' "Dead" woman casts vote for right to stay alive', *Sunday Times*, 7 January.

MacIntyre, A. (1981) *After Virtue*, London: Duckworth.

McCullagh, P. (1987) *The Foetus as Transplant Donor: Scientific, Social and Ethical Perspectives*, Chichester: John Wiley.

—— (1993) *Brain Dead, Brain Absent, Brain Donors*, Chichester: John Wiley.

Makhorn, S. K. and Dolan, W. V. (1981) 'Sexual assault and pregnancy', in T. W. Hilgers, D. J. Horan and D. Mall (eds) *New Perspectives on Human Abortion*, Frederick MD: University Publications of America.

Oderberg, D. (1997) 'Voluntary euthanasia and justice', in D. Oderberg and J. Laing (eds) *Human Lives: Critical Essays on Consequentialist Bioethics*, Basingstoke and London: Macmillan.

Rachels, J. (1979) 'Active and passive euthanasia', in J. Rachels (ed.) *Moral Problems: A Collection of Philosophical Essays*, 3rd edn, New York: Harper & Row.

Railton, P. (1988) 'Alienation, consequentialism, and the demands of morality', in S. Scheffler (ed.) *Consequentialism and its Critics*, New York: Oxford University Press.

Reardon, D. (1987) *Aborted Women: Silent No More*, Chicago: Loyola University Press.

—— (1996) *Making Abortion Rare: A Healing Strategy for a Divided Nation*, Springfield IL: Acorn Books.

Ryder, R. E. J. (1993) ' "Natural family planning": effective birth control supported by the Catholic Church', *British Medical Journal*, 307: 723–6. This article was followed by correspondence critical of Ryder (*British Medical Journal*, 307: 1003–5, 1360) and correspondence in support (*British Medical Journal*, 307: 1357–60).

Shewmon, D. A. (1997) 'Recovery from "brain death": a neurologist's *apologia*', *Linacre Quarterly*, 64, 1: 30–96.

—— (1998) ' "Brainstem death", "brain death" and death: a critical re-evaluation of the purported equivalence', *Issues in Law and Medicine*, 14, 2: 125–45.

Singer, P. (1993) *Practical Ethics*, 2nd edn, Cambridge: Cambridge University Press.

—— (1994) *Rethinking Life and Death*, Melbourne: The Text Publishing Company.

Singer, P. and Dawson, K. (1988) 'IVF technology and the argument from potential', *Philosophy and Public Affairs*, 17: 87–104; reprinted in P. Singer, H. Kuhse *et al.* (eds) (1990) *Embryo Experimentation*, Cambridge: Cambridge University Press.

Smart, J. J. C. (1973) 'An outline of a system of utilitarian ethics', in J. J. C. Smart and B. Williams (eds) *Utilitarianism: For and Against*, Cambridge: Cambridge University Press.

Smith, J. (1993) *Why Humanae Vitae Was Right: A Reader*, San Francisco: Ignatius.

Spencer, C. (1997) 'Obstinate questionings: an experience of abortion', in A. Kennedy (ed.) *Swimming against the Tide: Feminist Dissent on the Issue of Abortion*, Dublin: Open Air.

Stabile, I. (1996) *Ectopic Pregnancies: Diagnosis and Management*, Cambridge: Cambridge University Press.

Suarez, A. (1990) 'Hydatiform moles and teratomas confirm the human identity of the preimplantation embryo', *Journal of Medicine and Philosophy*, 15, 6: 627–35.

Sulmasy, D. P. and Sugarman, J. (1994) 'Are withholding and withdrawing therapy morally equivalent?', *Journal of Medical Ethics*, 20, 4: 218–22.

Thomson, J. J. (1971) 'A defense of abortion', *Philosophy and Public Affairs*, 1, 1; reprinted in M. Cohen, T. Nagel and T. Scanlon (eds) (1974) *The Rights and Wrongs of Abortion*, Princeton: Princeton University Press.

Tonti-Filippini, N. (1992) 'Further comments on the beginning of life', *Linacre Quarterly*, 59: 76–81.

Tooley, M. (1972) 'Abortion and infanticide', *Philosophy and Public Affairs*, 2, 1: 37–65; reprinted with amendments in M. Cohen, T. Nagel and T. Scanlon (eds) (1974) *The Rights and Wrongs of Abortion*, Princeton: Princeton University Press.

—— (1983) *Abortion and Infanticide*, New York: Oxford University Press.

Twycross, R. (1994) *Pain Relief in Advanced Cancer*, Edinburgh: Churchill Livingstone.

Wade, F. C. (1975) 'Potentiality in the abortion discussion', *Review of Metaphysics*, 29: 239–55.

Watt, H. (1996a) 'Potential and the early human', *Journal of Medical Ethics*, 22: 222–6.

—— (1996b) 'Ordinary and extraordinary means of prolonging life', *Medical Ethics and Bioethics*, 3, 3: 12–14.

—— (1998) 'Moral integrity in medical practice', in J. Glasa and J. R. Klepanec (eds) *Health Care Under Stress: Moral Integrity in Time of Scarcity*, Bratislava: Institute of Medical Ethics and Bioethics.

—— (in preparation) 'What constitutes direct abortion?'.

Wilks, J. (1997) *A Consumer's Guide to the Pill and other Drugs*, 2nd edn, Stafford VA: ALL Inc.

Williams, B. (1973) 'A critique of utilitarianism', in J. J. C. Smart and B. Williams (eds) *Utilitarianism: For and Against*, Cambridge: Cambridge University Press.

—— (1985) *Ethics and the Limits of Philosophy*, London: Fontana Press/Collins.

Zolese, G. and Blacker, C. V. R. (1992) 'The psychological complications of therapeutic abortion', *British Journal of Psychiatry*, 160: 742–9.

Index

Arthur case 5–6, 8–9, 11, 17, 28
autonomy 31, 32–3, 35–6; *see also* desires; intention

babies *see* infants; children
basic human goods *see* human goods
Beckwith, F.J. 79
benefits *see* human goods; interests
benefits of treatment *see* treatment
Benn, P. 73, 75
best interests *see* interests
birth 46, 48, 50, 59, 81
Blacker, C.V.R. 80, 81
Bland case 19–24, 27, 28
body 58, 79; lethal invasion of 41–2, 47, 51, 54, 55, 56, 79; and relationship to person 21–2, 47–8, 76; rights over 46–7, 51, 53–6; support by 46–7, 51, 52, 54, 56; *see also* human being; organism
Borthwick, C. 20
Boyes, Lilian 28, 29, 30, 31, 78
Boyle, J. 10, 78
brain damage 1, 19, 21, 26–7, 49, 50, 63, 79–80; *see also* coma; persistent vegetative state
brain death 19, 62–3, 76
brain life 62–3
Braine, D. 76
breastfeeding 46–7
Brody, B. 62
burdens of treatment *see* treatment
Byrne, P. 76

capacities 9, 10, 21, 22, 25, 49–50, 76–7, 79–80; self-organizing 50, 59, 61, 62–3, 78; *see also* potential
care 36, 77; basic nursing 25, 26, 77; duty of 20; goal of 24–5, 26–7; intensive 37; 'nursing care only'

5, 8; palliative *see* palliative care; significance of 26–7
Chang, R. 75
character *see* moral character
children 5, 6, 7, 8, 11, 12–13, 14, 26, 45, 47, 48, 49, 51–2, 53, 58, 59, 64, 69, 74, 81, 82; killing of 7–8, 51, 52, 55–6, 63, 70, 75, 80; respect for 48–52, 63; *see also* infants
chimeras 81
choice *see* actions; intention
cloning 1, 60, 62, 64–5, 82
coma 9, 19, 49; *see also* brain damage; consciousness
competent patient *see* patients
conception *see* fertilization
conceptus 60, 63, 82; *see also* embryo; hydatiform mole
conscientious objection *see* cooperation
consciousness 19, 20, 21, 22, 23, 24, 25, 26, 30, 49, 77; *see also* capacities
consequentialism 3, 11–16, 28, 43–4, 75–6; definition of 12, 43, 74, 75, 76; and infanticide 12–13, 75; objections to 13–16, 43–4, 75, 76
contraception 65, 82
cooperation 67–71, 82–3; formal 68, 69, 83; material 68, 69, 70, 71, 83
Cox case 28, 29–31, 78
Crisp, R. 79

Davis, A. 78
Dawson, K. 61
death: as benefit 31, 32, 77; causing/hastening 5, 6–8, 17, 20, 24, 25, 27–8, 30, 31–2, 34–44, 46–7, 51–6, 57–8, 64–5, 73, 74, 75, 79, 82; definition/diagnosis 19, 62–3, 76, 77, 81; effects of 14, 75, 76, 77, 80; intended 5, 6–8, 17, 20, 24, 25, 27–8, 30, 34,